Dr. Denmark
Said It!

Dr. Denmark
Said It!

Advice to Mothers
From America's Most
Experienced Pediatrician

Madia L. Bowman

ISBN: 0–9703814–0–9

Cover design and layout by Terri Lynn Fike

The ideas, procedures, and suggestions in this book are
intended to supplement, not replace, the medical advice of
a trained professional. All matters regarding your health
require medical supervision. Consult your physician before
adopting the suggestions in this book, as well as concerning any condition that may require diagnosis or medical
attention. The author disclaims any liability arising directly,
or indirectly, from the use of, this book.

In loving memory of Mr. John Eustace Denmark,
without whose encouragement and support Dr. Denmark's
ministry to little folks would never have been possible.
Also in memory of my father, Rev. Hugh MacIntyre Linton.
His example in sanctified optimism and unswerving
dedication to his work helped me finish this book.

Older women likewise are to be reverent in
their behavior, not malicious gossips, nor enslaved
to much wine, teaching what is good, that they may
encourage the young women to love their husbands,
to love their children, to be sensible, pure, workers at
home, kind, being subject to their own husbands,
that the word of God may not be dishonored.

Titus 2:3–5

Contents

Acknowledgments

When I started this book my son David was a newborn. We celebrated his eighth birthday a week after the text was complete. God has good reasons for keeping the future a secret. If I had known the extent of this project or that David would have five younger siblings, I would never have attempted it.

Miraculously, the book was finished and now a second edition is available. I thank God for the vision and the resources necessary to carry it this far. So many people have encouraged and helped. Marlene Goodrum shared this vision in its seed form, patiently deciphered my scribbling, and typed the earliest draft. Cathy Hoffer helped in a myriad of ways: proofreading, brainstorming, advising, and contacting publishers. Lynn Holman spent countless hours typing and revamping. I want to thank Mary Hutcherson (Dr. Denmark's daughter) and Julia Lee Dulfer for reviewing and editing. My husband Steve also shared the vision and wrote Dr. Denmark's biographical sketch.

The work couldn't have continued had it not been for my older daughters, Malinda and Jessica, who looked after the little ones while I was writing. Jessica also helped put together the index. Katie Fearon and Sarah Pitts babysat when my daughters were unavailable. I cannot forget the moms who took the time to write the testimonials, many of which are included in chapter fourteen.

There were so many others who helped, advised, and encouraged: my brother Andy Linton, my mom Betty Linton, Traci Clanton, Nora Pitts, Tim and Windy Echols with Family Resource Network, Suzanne and Larry Miller, Creston Mapes, Jim Vitti, Paula Lewis, and Terri Lynn Fike. Without Gary DeMar of American Vision, this book might never have come to completion. He helped tremendously in the final stages of preparing the manuscript for publication.

Last, but not least, I cannot fail to thank Dr. Denmark. She has cared for my children and mentored me for twenty-one years. I am grateful for her example, wisdom and willingness to cooperate with this project. Thank you, Dr. "D"! Thank you, everyone!

Foreword

By Robert A. Rohm, Ph.D.*

Little Rachael Anne Rohm, our first child, was born July 31, 1973. Neither her mother, nor I, knew what we were about to face. Children are a blessing from the Lord, but that does not make the task of parenting any easier. It is indeed a first class challenge...especially when your firstborn arrives and you feel totally unprepared. The only real help comes from reading "baby books", listening to relatives and calling other trusted friends. In addition to all that, proper child rearing is a delicate issue with many people, especially *new* parents.

Rachael dominated our every waking and non-waking moment. When she cried, we jumped! We had heard that when a child cried, it had a need. It did not take her long to have a lot of needs! She seemed to never sleep, wanted to feed on demand, and was just irritable in general. We loved her dearly, but really questioned our ability in being up to the task of parenting her.

Then one day a lady family friend told us about this special, unusual pediatrician by the name of Dr. Leila Denmark. (Looking back, I can see that our friend understood our dilemma better than we did. We only understood the problem, but she actually understood the solution!)

---

*Dr. Robert A. Rohm is president of Personality Insights in Atlanta, Georgia.

We went to see Dr. Denmark. After an introduction and a few preliminaries, Dr. Denmark looked at us and said, "Did you move in with the baby, or did the baby move in with you?" She then proceeded to explain the importance of a schedule and routine and the fact that at times babies *needed* to cry in order to get exercise (provided they had been fed and were clean). I liked the way she spoke with certainty. Her wisdom, "horse sense", professional manner, caring attitude and compassion for child and parent alike sold us immediately. Needless to say, in time some marvelous changes began to occur.

As the years passed, we had three more children. Their first years were so different, so pleasant! It was the difference between day and night. We had learned so very much from this wise medical doctor. Bringing home and caring for newborns actually became a pleasant experience. In addition to all this, I know for a fact all of our children were a lot healthier, too. Rachael, who had often been sick with routine illnesses, began to be healthy. The other children were healthier as well. It is amazing how much money we were able to save in unnecessary health care costs.

Dr. Denmark has not only been a real friend to "little people" as she refers to them, but she has also been a lifeline to parents. Quite frankly, I do not know what we would have done without her.

As you read the wisdom contained in these pages, you will silently thank God for the excellent work Madia Bowman has accomplished. Her eight years in researching, writing, and focusing on Dr. Denmark's thoughts and philosophies will save you time, effort, and a lot of unnecessary heartache. Dr. Denmark is a very special person. Since she has recently passed the century mark in age, now seems to be a fitting time to put her excellent opinions and remedies in writing.

Read, enjoy, marvel, but most of all apply. You and your child will be the winners for it. God bless you!

Introduction

Rearing children is the most important work on earth.
There's nothing like it. It's the hardest job and the
biggest one. It should be the most elevated.

—Leila Denmark

If someday you happen to be driving through the pretty countryside around Alpharetta, Georgia, and find yourself on Highway 9, drive north. Look for Midway Methodist Church on the right; you can't miss it. When you come to Midway, you have just crossed the Forsyth County line. It's where we Bowmans live and where Dr. Leila Denmark practices medicine.

Just exploring? Stop by Dr. D.'s for a moment and breathe the fresh air under the spreading oaks. If by chance your little one isn't feeling well, stay and see her. Patients don't come by appointment. Everybody takes his turn. No matter how long you might have to wait, it's worth it.

For over seventy years thousands of children have been lovingly treated by Dr. Denmark. Their concerned, confused, and tired mothers have benefited from her advice. They come away encouraged, admonished, with practical suggestions for tending ailing youngsters and wise counsel for living.

In our fast-changing culture, moms can become thoroughly confused by conflicting information. Modern child psychology, trendy pediatrics, and shifting views on nutrition contribute to frustrated parenting.

Dr. Denmark offers a breath of sanity in the midst of confusion. She encourages mothers to "look for the obvious" and "use their own minds," thus guiding them through the maze of advice from so-called experts. Best of all, her counsel is time tested.

In 1990 I determined to compile some of Dr. Denmark's medical wisdom. My original goal was to add an appendix to her book, *Every Child Should Have a Chance.* When approached about the project, she had another idea.

"Mrs. Bowman, you take what I've said and write it down. Add some of your own insights. You're the mother of six (now ten) children. You know something. Write your own book." She paused thoughtfully, "Maybe you can help somebody." So that's what I've done.

Unless otherwise specified, all the medical advice contained herein comes directly from Dr. Denmark. Medications, treatments, daily routines, and diets are her recommendations. I've included a number of personal letters that attest to their practicality. As for the child-rearing philosophy, it's my own, developed through study of the Bible and personal experience as well as numerous conversations with Dr. Denmark. I hope you will enjoy her words of wisdom appearing in bold italics throughout the text.

I also hope and pray this book will indeed "help somebody."

Care of 1 Infants

On January 9, 1980, a young woman sat in the waiting room of Dr. Leila Denmark's office holding her first child, a two-day-old baby girl.

The new mother's emotions ranged from bewilderment to awe to trepidation as she gazed at her daughter's tiny face. In her arms lay a great blessing...and an overwhelming responsibility. Her own mother was thousands of miles away in a foreign country, unavailable for day-to-day counsel. She so wanted to be a good parent and do everything right.

Friends recommended Dr. Denmark. Could an eighty-two-year-old pediatrician be that capable? Had she made the right decision in coming?

She didn't know what an impact that appointment would have upon her child-rearing experience. Nine children later, she remembers and is thankful. I am that woman, and Dr. Denmark remains my mentor. She is still a great blessing to our family.

A child is a precious gift, divinely given. Nothing is more helpless than a newborn, who is completely dependent on his parents' care. The advent of a baby into the home can bring a frenzied, sleepless, and trying time or be a precious experience filled with peace and wonder. A few principles of child care can make all the difference. New parents need wise counsel so that mother, father, and baby get off to the best start possible.

When I was a young doctor, I used to meet with new parents at the hospital after the baby arrived. Often grandparents came too. The first thing I said to the mother was, "This baby has come to live with you, not you with the baby. He needs to be trained into a system. If you were building an important business, you'd have a system, and building a human being is the most critical thing on earth. You're going to die one day and leave this little creature here. If you haven't built him a way of life, somebody's going to kick him around. That's the reason our jails are so full today. Those people didn't have a chance because they didn't have parents who taught them a way of life.

The day that baby was conceived, everything was in one cell: its height, color, disposition, its whole life. If you took care of yourself during pregnancy—didn't drink, smoke, do drugs, or drink too much milk—at birth that baby is all it was meant to be. Now, if you don't feed him right and look after him properly until he's eighteen years old, he can never reach his full potential. This little baby has to have a system. There should be a time for everything.

You will have everybody on earth telling you how to rear your child. I'm telling you, your mother-in law's telling you, all your neighbors are going to tell you how to do it. Listen carefully to what everybody says and reply, "Yes, ma'am; yes, sir," and go home and do just what you think is best.

Newborn

Schedules

A good routine of eating and sleeping is vital for the health of the child and for family harmony. Upon returning from the hospital, a mother should put her newborn on a consistent schedule of eating and sleeping. The following is recommended:

6:00 a.m.   Feed breast milk or formula; allow baby to sleep in an open room. Raise the window shades and leave the door ajar if there is no danger of a toddler harming the baby.

9:30 a.m.   Bathe

10:00 a.m.   Feed and put down for nap with door and shades closed. Assure quiet.

2:00 p.m.   Feed, leaving the room open, and play with baby.

6:00 p.m.   Feed

10:00 p.m.   Feed. Change diaper; check to see if baby is all right.*

*   Do not pick the child up or feed him until 6:00 a.m.

If an infant is fed too frequently he becomes colicky and spits up. His stomach is not empty when new food is added. Proper digestion becomes impossible, resulting in a very distended, painful stomach.

Crying Infant

Before a child is acclimated to the above schedule, he will most likely cry and want to be fed during the night. It won't hurt him to cry. After a few days most babies become accustomed to the schedule and begin sleeping through the night. Mother, father, and baby receive needed rest. Actually, it is absolutely necessary that a newborn infant cry. Crying is nature's way of expanding and strengthening his lungs. A newborn generally sleeps twenty hours out of twenty-four. He may spend up to four hours crying every day.

Many experienced moms recommend keeping baby awake as much as possible between the six and ten o'clock feedings so he is more likely to sleep throughout the night. Bring him into the living room and play gently with him. If it is not too noisy this would be a good time for other family members to interact with him as well. Bear in mind however, that a newborn will snooze off and on throughout the day.

Some infants take longer than others to begin sleeping through the night. If your baby is one of those ask yourself, "Am I following the schedule consistently? (Consistency is vital.) Is my baby positioned so that he feels secure (see Positioning, pages 11–12)? Am I keeping his bedroom quiet? Do I need to exercise self-control and persevere a few more nights?"

Use your discretion remembering that normal, healthy infants do cry even if nothing is wrong. Many things can wake a baby up. Check for fever, a stuffy nose, diaper rash, or abnormal bowel movements. Is baby gaining normally?

After ruling out the above you might try giving him a little formula at ten o'clock after you nurse him. You may be tired and not producing enough milk in the evening. Mix one tablespoon of powdered formula with two ounces of sterile water (yielding two ounces of formula).

If he drinks the entire amount, feed him two and one half ounces the next night after nursing. Continue increasing the amount every night by one half ounce until he leaves a little in the bottle An infant will not drink too much. Minor supplementing may be all it takes to help baby sleep until six (see Supplements, pages 8–9).

As a new mother I loved cuddling my baby but it was a tremendous relief to me to realize I didn't have to pick her up every time she cried. I noticed that she fell asleep sooner at bedtime when I let her fuss a while.

If there is truly something wrong a mother should respond. However don't get in the habit of "pacifying" your child. Today pacifying is picking him up whenever he cries. Tomorrow he will want cookies, and in his teens it will be a car. Pacifying is a costly habit in many respects (see pages 179–180, 180–181).

We worry about premature babies and those with Down syndrome because they don't cry enough.

Feeding

Breast Feeding

Nurse your baby if possible. It contributes to the mother's and especially the baby's good health. A nursing mother should eat plenty of whole grains and leafy, green vegetables and drink lots of water and soups (no milk or juice); and be happy.

Nurse your baby ten minutes on each side, burping him at the change over and after nursing. When on the first breast, press the nipple of the opposite breast to keep its milk from flowing.

After nursing, wash the baby's saliva off your breasts with clear water (no soap), dry them, and put clean cotton fabric between the nipples and bra. The cleansing is especially important while your nipples are becoming acclimated to nursing. Washing helps prevent (or treat) cracked, sore nipples. Note that thrush in the infant's mouth can also produce soreness (see Thrush, pages 15–16). If the nipples have become so badly cracked that there is actually a cut, you may apply Silvadene cream after each feeding.

Rinse it off with clear water before the next nursing. The residual Silvadene will not hurt baby.

Some people think that frequent and prolonged nursing increases milk supply. No, that doesn't do it at all. I had a woman in here the other day who was nursing her baby every two hours around the clock. She was worn out and looked like heck. The baby looked like the wrath of God, and the husband was ready to leave home! She didn't need to nurse her baby every two hours. The way to make milk is to be happy, have a system, and love to do it.

Supplements

The amount of milk a baby consumes is determined by his individual needs. If a child is gaining well and seems content, don't be concerned about the sufficiency of your breast milk. If the baby isn't gaining well and you're worried about his not getting enough, you can weigh him before and after nursing. During the first two weeks, most babies should weigh three to four ounces more after nursing. When he is six weeks old, he should weigh approximately eight ounces more after nursing. Most children continue to drink approximately eight ounces until they are weaned if pureed foods are introduced at the proper time.

If your child isn't receiving enough breast milk, you should supplement with formula, but always nurse first. (Otherwise your breast milk will quickly dry up.) After nursing, offer him however many ounces of formula he is lacking. For example, if your three-week-old gains only two ounces after nursing, offer him approximately two ounces of formula at the first feeding. If he drinks the entire amount increase it by one-half ounce at the next feeding. A baby won't drink too much formula. You can continue increasing the amount by half-ounces until he leaves a little in the bottle.

That way you can be certain he's receiving all he needs.

Try a cow's milk formula first. If the baby spits up constantly, has eczema or diarrhea, switch to a soybean formula (see Spitting Up, below). Keep trying until you find one that works. If you're using formula that is intended to be diluted with water, add a little more water than the directions indicate on the can until your baby is three months old. Instead of one can of water to one can of formula, use *one and one half* cans of water to one can of formula. After your baby is three months follow the directions on the can.

It is critical that the formula is warm and flows freely from the baby's bottle. If the nipple doesn't have a cross cut at the tip, make one yourself with a razor blade. Each cut should be approximately one sixteenth of an inch long. Hold the bottle firmly and provide some resistance to his sucking motion so he can pull on the nipple as he would pull on a breast nipple.

Although my figure is on the petite side, breast feeding was never much of a problem with our first seven children. Contrary to what many think, the size of a woman's breasts has very little to do with her ability to breast feed.

When Christina was born (number eight), however, I was unable to produce all she needed and had to supplement. She never nursed aggressively and finally at five months rejected the breast altogether. Initially my reaction was disappointment and grief. Somehow I felt like a failure, but my attitude changed. Hey, I wasn't a failure. Breast feeding is ideal, and I had been willing but just not able. Anyway, Christina was such a healthy, jolly little creature. Thank God for supplements when we need them! Thank God for healthy babies!

Spitting Up

Spitting up can be caused by too frequent feedings (see page 5), a food allergy, or a weak esophageal gastric valve. If a child spits up water in addition to formula, it's a good indication that he has a weak esophageal gastric valve, a normal condition in an infant. He may do it frequently for eight months but will gain normally.

Spitting up only formula or breast milk indicates a food allergy. Try changing the formula. As a nursing mother, you need to eliminate various foods from your diet to determine the cause. Common offenders are milk products, citrus, and chocolate.

Projectile vomiting, especially in males, is cause for serious concern. It's like an explosion: the entire meal returns, and you can detect a rise and fall in his stomach as he ejects the food. Consult a physician immediately.

It's nice when babies spit up. They don't have as many colds. Nobody wants to hold them!

Weight Gains

All newborns lose about eight ounces the first few days but should regain their birth weight after one week. From then on, infants usually gain one ounce daily until they are twelve weeks old (approximately two pounds a month). After that they drop down to gaining a half-ounce daily. At five months most infants have added approximately eight pounds to their birth weight.

One of the finest babies I ever had wouldn't eat over three ounces at a time. Babies do have individual needs. Consistent weight gain is what a mother should look for.

Postpartum

For your own sake as well as your infant's, don't be in a hurry to get back to a full schedule after giving birth. If you can get some help with household duties, take advantage of it. Rest as much as you can for at least two weeks to give your body a chance to recover. If you're nursing you need to let your milk get established. Staying quietly at home is best for both mother and baby.

When my child was born, I stayed in the hospital for two weeks. Then I went home, and somebody looked after me for two weeks. After that I took it kind of easy for a while. Maybe in the old days we overdid the recuperation period, but I do believe if you've been pregnant nine months you need some rest. You've lost some blood. Your abdominal muscles are weak, and everything is out of line. I think a mother should go slowly for about a month after delivery, especially if she plans to nurse.

If a mother gets up the day the baby's born and plans a banquet, she's weak, worn out, and likely out of sorts. If she wants to nurse, she must be happy. I think postpartum should be a time of peace. A woman needs time to get established before she tries to take over the whole shop again.

Positioning

Infants should always be placed on their stomachs for the first five months. They are safer and feel more secure in that position. An infant placed on his back flails his arms because he's afraid of falling. For months he has been enfolded in his mother's womb, but on his back, his limbs move too freely, so he feels insecure. He becomes startled, gasps, and takes in air that creates colic.

Leaving a baby on his back is potentially fatal. There is a constant danger that a child may spit up and asphyxiate himself if he's lying on his back. On his stomach, he's in no danger of choking on vomit. Towels placed under the sheet will absorb vomit, and the baby won't aspirate it into his lungs (see Furniture Use, below).

Sleeping on his stomach also helps the child develop a nicely shaped head. A child positioned on his back typically develops a head that is flat on the back. Putting him on his side may cause a lopsided shape to his head. An infant is better able to exercise his neck, shoulder, and arm muscles while on his stomach. It's also easier for him to have bowel movements and pass gas (see pages 186–187).

I've practiced medicine for over seventy years, and I've never had a crib death. I tell mothers, "The minute that baby's born, don't ever leave it on its back except to nurse it." (see Sudden Infant Death Syndrome, pages 166–167).

Furniture Use

Infant swings and modern car seats unfortunately are not good for the spine. The cartilage between the vertebrae is particularly soft in a newborn's back and he shouldn't be allowed to hunch over in the early months. It's best to keep him in his crib at home, spending minimal time in a car seat, especially before five or six months of age.

Making baby's bed properly is important. Spread four towels on the crib mattress and stretch a sheet tightly over them. This kind of surface contributes toward proper breathing and absorbs fluid. Never put your baby on a fluffy or furry-textured surface that might inhibit his breathing. Nor should you place him on a carpet even with a blanket beneath him. Carpets contain a host of allergens, and babies can develop nasal congestion and ear infections from them.

Quietness

A newborn may not always appear to be sensitive to noise. In reality he is very much affected by it. His eardrums are thin as tissue paper, and any sound he previously received through the amniotic fluid was muffled.

You'll want to protect your infant from unnecessarily loud noises, especially respecting sleeptime. Keep the room as quiet as possible and allow minimal visitors, particularly during the first five months. Turn off the TV and the radio. If there's a telephone in the room, turn off the ringer.

It is unfortunate when mothers are in a hurry to take their infants into public. They need a quiet life away from the bustle of the outside world, particularly during those first five months. Exposing them to crowds increases the probability of their becoming sick, which can interfere with the rapid growth that is crucial at this time.

A little newborn has few immunities. If you take him to church and put him in the nursery on Sunday, I'll probably see him on Wednesday. Why? Because somebody brought a sick baby to the nursery and he was coughed on.

Feet and Shoes

Every baby is born with crooked feet. They turn in or out depending on how he was positioned in his mother's womb.

Typically, a child born with turned-in feet will walk sooner than one born with turned-out feet. Except in extreme cases such as clubbed feet, they will straighten out by themselves and need no orthopedic care. Babies really don't need shoes in the early months. He needs to use his feet, and it's easier for him to walk if he's barefooted.

When I first started practicing medicine, we spent a world of money on night splints and special shoes. I found that if left alone, by age two the baby's feet would straighten out by themselves. If they're not straight by then I have the mother buy roller skates and let baby skate a few minutes a day. It's a great way to train the feet to toe straight ahead.

My own grandchild didn't own a pair of shoes until he was one and a half. I went to see him one time, and he said to me, "Dr. Leila, I'm so proud of my little black shoes!"

Sunshine

By the time your baby is two weeks old, take him outside for about five minutes a day. Lift his shirt and let the sun shine on his back. It will satisfy his requirement for vitamin D.

Jaundice

When the skin or the whites of the eyes seem unusually yellow in color, a child may be considered jaundiced. If your baby appears jaundiced, first check the color of his stools and urine. White stools and tea-colored urine mean no bile is coming through the bile duct. He needs the immediate attention of a physician. Normal urine and stools indicate your baby is probably just fine and needs no treatment. Sunlamps are not necessary, and he should not be taken off the breast.

A newborn can become jaundiced if the mother is anemic during pregnancy. The oxygen he received came through her blood via the placenta. If she was anemic, the oxygen level was low, and the child had to build as many red blood cells as possible in order to pick up whatever oxygen was afforded him. His system manufactured far more red blood cells than he needed after birth. The extra cells are then destroyed, causing jaundice, which usually disappears after a few days.

Anemia in pregnancy is commonly caused by overconsumption of dairy products (see anemia, pages 122, 125–126).

Pacifiers and Thrush

Babies should not be given pacifiers; it's much better for them to suck their fingers or thumbs. Those who use pacifiers may develop a fungus called thrush. White in color, it looks like curdled milk and covers the tongue, throat, cheeks, and roof of the mouth.

Breast nipples are soft and gentle. Sucking the rough rubber of a pacifier, interferes with the epithelial cells in the baby's mouth and can cause growth of the fungus that produces thrush. If just the top of the baby's tongue looks white and other parts of his mouth don't, he probably doesn't have it. He may simply be sleeping with his mouth open. To treat thrush put Mycostatin suspension on a Q-tip and rub it on the insides of the cheeks, roof of the mouth, and under the lips after each feeding.

Never use water in a bottle as a pacifier. If your drowsy baby keeps sucking and you keep filling the bottle, excess water can dilute the baby's electrolytes (see Drinks, pages 123–125).

A pacifier is a dirty thing. It is put down in places one would never put a toothbrush and then placed back in the baby's mouth. There are germs and fungus in the house. A pacifier is nasty, but it does help the economy, and the doctor needs a job!

Diaper Rash

Mild diaper rash appears as a slight redness. More severe rashes are fiery red and pimply and may even have blisters similar to those of a burn. Its three most common causes are antibiotics, alkaline urine (often a result of drinking juice), and allergic reaction. A severe rash is the result of an allergic reaction developing into a fungus infection.

Don't use baby wipes. For the first six months, keep a bottle of sterile water next to the crib. Wipe the baby's bottom with cotton dipped in it.

Even a mild diaper rash is uncomfortable and can worsen, so it should be treated immediately. Try removing the diaper and allowing more air to get to the baby's skin. (You will have to change bedding frequently.) Also try to determine the cause of the allergic reaction that is producing the rash. Possible causes might be a particular detergent used to wash the diaper or a food you're eating that the baby is reacting to through your breast milk. Don't give the baby juices.

If you are using disposable diapers, you may need to switch to another brand. Consider using cloth diapers. Disposables are very airproof and keep the baby's skin at a higher temperature than cloth diapers do, thereby contributing to fungus growth.

For a severe diaper rash, indicating a fungal infection, keep the area as dry as possible and apply Mycostatin powder three times a day. If the skin becomes raw and/or blistered, use Silvad-ene cream three times a day in addition to the Mycostatin. Apply the cream first and sprinkle powder on top. No other cream or ointment should be used with severe diaper rash.

Teething

Many generations of American women believed in "teething." We have been told that it can cause irritability and even fever in our infants. Two generations ago infants' gums were even lanced to reduce the pain. Dr. Denmark rejects this notion of teething. She says, "A child actually begins to teethe five months after conception and continues to do so for eighteen years with no symptoms."

Three Months

Schedules

6:00 a.m. Nurse
10:00 a.m. Nurse and feed. Nap.
2:00 p.m. Nurse and feed. Play time.
6:00 p.m. Nurse and feed. Put to bed
10:00 p.m. Nurse and put to bed for the night.

At twelve weeks you may notice your child stays awake longer, doesn't cry as long, and has begun drooling. Drooling is an indication that the child's saliva now contains ptyalin, the enzyme that enables him to change starch into sugar. It's time to begin slowly introducing foods into his diet. The drooling stops when he learns to swallow his saliva. If his nose is stopped up, he may drool indefinitely.

The nursing schedule remains the same (6—10—2—6—10), but you may now offer pureed foods after nursing at 10—2—6.

Try one new kind of food at a time and observe the infant over the next four days for any signs of allergic reaction. During that time give him one-fourth teaspoon of the new food per meal.

If no reaction occurs you can assume there is no allergy and begin to increase the amount of tested food. Now add another new food, one-fourth teaspoon at a time for four days. It's a safe way to introduce your baby to a large variety of foods, and you will detect any allergies early.

Should an allergic reaction occur, write down the particular food that caused it and a description of the reaction. It might manifest itself as a rash, diarrhea, asthma, eczema, vomiting, hay fever, a clear running nose, or excessive crying. Any abnormal condition should be recorded. Try the food in question one month later and check for a similar reaction. Introduce the food three times at one-month intervals. If the reaction occurs each time, you may assume that the child has a lifetime allergy to it.

Until they become acclimated to its new texture, many infants spit out most of the food. Some babies are easier to feed than others, but in any case be patient and keep trying. Have fun and enjoy the new experience with him.

Rice cereal, applesauce, and bananas are good to start off with. Next introduce vegetables and meat. Mix everything together. Your baby is accustomed to the warm sweet taste of breast milk or formula, so he is more likely to accept it if it's served warm and sweetened with fruit. Give him as much as he wants. After a while you may be surprised at how much he will eat.

Commercially produced baby food is fine (see page 22). If you make it at home, be sure it is well pureed and boiled for three minutes before serving.

Always offer the breast before food. Bottle feedings come after food. If you're supplementing your breast milk, nurse first, give pureed foods second, and bottle feed last. That order is more conducive to success. A supplementing mother should mix as much formula with the pureed food as possible.

Baby food has done more for little people than anything except immunizations. Until about seventy-five years ago, mothers chewed for their children. The baby ate everything off her plate. Then we learned about germs, and mothers quit doing it. Babies couldn't chew for themselves and didn't get the nutrients they needed. So many developed scurvy, rickets, sprue — all kinds of deficiency diseases. People began to rub Campbell's vegetable soup through a sieve, and it worked like magic. One poor old man, a Mr. Clapp (I went hiking with him once in the Smokies), had a sick wife who couldn't digest food well, so he began sieving and canning it for her. He got the idea of making baby food that way and selling it. Then we went to heaven!

Homemade Baby Food

Dr. Denmark's baby-food plan has worked wonderfully for all of our ten children. Mixing the various food types with plenty of fruit as a sweetener is an excellent way to ensure that baby receives a balance of all the necessary nutrients. The mixture sounds and looks disgusting, but our infants have loved it and thrived on it.

I usually begin them on commercial rice cereal mixed with expressed breast milk, then progress to bananas and other fruit and eliminate the milk. After fruit I usually add carrots or squash. Proteins come last.

When my babies are eating small amounts, I use store-bought food for convenience. Dr. Denmark assured me that's fine if it's the right kind (see page 22). However, anyone who has priced it at the grocery store knows the expense involved in using it regularly. After my babies are eating more I normally make my own. The following tips may be helpful.

Invest in a good food processor. There is no doubt our Cuisinart has saved us thousands of dollars.

Make sure all food is well cooked and mixed with enough water to yield a smooth consistency when pureed. I usually make mine slightly thicker than the store-bought variety. Most babies don't like lumps and can choke on large ones. Be sure to blend or strain them out. Use well ripened, sliced bananas.

Avoid using salty or spicy foods. I try to rinse out salt if I'm using canned foods and remove home-cooked vegetables before adding salt for the rest of the family.

When in doubt throw it out. Make sure all food is fresh. Don't keep it in the refrigerator too long. Babies' stomachs are especially sensitive to bacteria. It's probably best to boil it just before serving, especially for young infants.

Some mothers make a week's worth of food at a time and freeze it in ice cube trays until needed. Others fix a couple of days' worth and keep it in the refrigerator. I generally make enough for two or three meals, pureeing the same food I have cooked for the rest of the family. Use whichever system you find most convenient.

Four Months

Schedules

If a child starts with pureed foods at twelve weeks according to Dr. Denmark's system, his consumption should increase rapidly. He'll be ready to start a three-meal schedule. Nurse before each feeding.

7:00 a.m.   Nurse and feed.

9:00 a.m.   Bathe and put down for a three-hour nap.

12:30 p.m. Nurse and feed; play in the afternoon (no scheduled nap).

6:00 p.m.   Nurse, feed, and put to bed (should sleep until morning).

Breakfast

- 2 tablespoons fruit
- 3 tablespoons protein
- 3 tablespoons starch
- 1 banana

All of the above should be well pureed, mixed together, boiled for three minutes, and served warm. It's best to serve the food right out of the pot to reduce the possibility of contamination.

Lunch

- 2 tablespoons fruit
- 3 tablespoons protein
- 3 tablespoons starch
- 3 tablespoons vegetables
- 1 banana

Supper

- Same as lunch

Acceptable proteins are lean meat, eggs, or black-eyed peas. Other beans may be used occasionally, but black-eyed peas are the superior legume because of their high protein content.

Leafy or green vegetables are best to use because of their high iron content. Other vegetables may be interspersed with them. Commercially produced baby food is fine, but always purchase unmixed varieties. Combination foods contain too much starch. For example, buy beef and carrots in separate jars, not as beef stew.

Your child shouldn't have juice or any other beverage.

Naptime

At four months a baby no longer needs a scheduled afternoon nap. He may catnap on his own in the playpen or car seat but should begin weaning himself from sleeping in the afternoon. Encourage him to stay awake by keeping him in the living room or kitchen so he can watch family activity and play with his toys.

Five Months

Food, Schedules, Sleep

Diet, mealtime, and sleeptime are identical to the four-month schedule, but now begin giving him small sips of water from a cup. There's never any need to give it in a bottle. It takes practice, but they can learn to drink from a cup at an early age.

Don't give a child mashed or whole food until eight molars develop at approximately twenty-eight months (development is individual). Food should be well pureed, or it can irritate the stomach.

When baby is old enough to discover his food differs from that of the rest of the family, it sometimes causes a struggle. He wants to eat what everyone else has. Remember, he doesn't have the discernment to realize it's hard for his stomach to handle unchewed, unpureed food. Resist the temptation to give in and allow him to eat what he wants. If he rejects food at one meal, don't become upset; merely wait until the next. Even the appetites of healthy babies may vary. After he's had mashed food it is difficult to revert to puree. He will do it, though, when he learns that is all he'll get!

When old people lose their teeth they spend a lot of money to buy new ones. They don't just mash food up and swallow it—it makes them sick.

It's just like a country girl seeing electric lights—she's not going to want to wash lamp shades any more. Once a child has tasted mashed food from the table, he thinks he has to eat like his parents, but he can't digest it properly until he has something to chew it with. It comes out in the diaper as it goes in.

Convinced that it was better to delay giving table food, I tried various tactics to avoid a battle. Two things seemed particularly effective: Feeding baby before the rest of the family eats and not giving him anything that would whet his appetite for table food—crackers, cookies, Cheerios.

Don't give your baby juice, carbonated drinks, or snacks between meals (see Drinks, pages 123–125).

Children who eat between meals get potbellied, anemic, and sorry. Their stomachs never have a chance to empty, so they're always hungry but never hungry enough to eat a decent meal. A hog will eat a lot and stretch out to rest until it digests its food. Then it will eat some more. Even a hog's got enough sense to eat right. A cow, of course, has two stomachs so can eat all day.

If children come to my clinic with pot bellies and dry, thin hair, I always ask their mother if she feeds them between meals. If the mother says no, I check the soles of their shoes for crumbs. Finding any means there is probably snack food strewn all over the house. Eating between meals is so chaotic.

You see big pot bellies on old people with the same eating patterns. They could be nice neat people if they just ate three simple meals a day and stayed out of the doctor's office.

The three major causes of tooth decay are eating between meals, carbonated drinks, and mouth breathing.

Weaning

Dr. Denmark stresses that infants need to be weaned at seven months. By then they should be eating plenty of pureed food and taking sips of water from a cup. Most breast-fed babies never need a bottle and can be weaned directly to a cup (see Drinks, pages 123–125). After weaning you don't need to add milk or formula to his diet. It can produce anemia. Milk also decreases his appetite for other vital foods (see Dairy Products, pages 125–127).

Offer babies and children water at every meal but don't worry if they refuse unless they are sick. Pureed foods contain a lot of water and your baby may not need to drink after eating. If your child is sick, refusing food, or the weather is especially hot, do carefully monitor his fluid intake (see Further Information on Preventing Dehydration, pages 58–59).

Sleep

When baby is trained to expect a consistent nap schedule, he'll be happy in bed even if he doesn't sleep the entire time. Remember to pull down the shades, close the door, and keep things as quiet as possible. Put a safe "friend" (doll, blanket, or toy animal) in with him at naptime and at night. It's good for him to be attached to a particular toy. Some children need less sleep and will wake up during naps or at night and play with it in the crib. That's fine and it enables you to do necessary household chores.

Morning is a better time for a nap. When baby sleeps in the morning and is awake all afternoon, he's tired and ready for bed shortly after supper.

Most children on a regular schedule won't object to staying in their cribs from 9:00 to 12:00. It's a routine that adds peace to the household.

If parents put their children to bed at a sensible hour, eventually they begin sleeping at the right time. Afternoon nappers are usually not good night sleepers. It's important for baby to go to bed early enough so mama and papa can have a break in the evening.

When I was a young, inexperienced doctor, a mother brought her two little daughters into my clinic and claimed it was impossible to get them to bed. She wanted me to prescribe a sedative for them.

I was puzzled and kept questioning her to determine the cause of her children's sleeplessness. Finally, I asked, "What time do they get up in the morning?"

"About 11:30," she responded.

"Well then, they shouldn't go to bed until 11:30 p.m.!" I told the mother. I advised her to get them up at 7 and give them breakfast. If she did that they would be ready to go to bed at the right time.

Dr. Denmark's recommended morning nap schedule has been invaluable to our family life. I follow it pretty strictly, so my babies come to expect it. Those three hours are precious and I use them to accomplish any task that requires concentration (paperwork, children's studies, important phone calls). I'm not sure I could manage the home with any semblance of order if it were otherwise. I do encourage my little ones to stay up in the afternoon so they are definitely ready for bed by evening. I too am ready for them to go!

Two Years

A two-year old's the cutest thing there is. They say "I do," and they mean it.

Food, Schedules, Sleep
  7:00 a.m.   Breakfast
12:30 p.m.   Lunch
  6:00 p.m.   Supper

At twenty-four months, a child's appetite typically drops drastically. Growth slows, and he will begin eating about a fifth as much as before. The change is normal.

Continue the four-month menu, giving him only water to drink. Fruit at meals is highly preferable to fruit juice. No snacks.

At this age a child no longer needs a daytime nap and will sleep approximately twelve hours until he is six years old. Eliminating the naps will help him sleep earlier and better, and parents and older children can enjoy a quiet evening!

I encourage my toddlers to have a "quiet time" in the morning when they are no longer napping. They usually sit down with books or toys. Quiet time enables older home-schooled siblings to concentrate better on their studies and helps the younger ones sleep more soundly.

Baby Schedule Summary

Birth to Three Months

6:00 a.m.	Feed (breast or bottle): sleep in open room
9:30 a.m.	Bathe
10:00 a.m.	Feed (breast or bottle): nap and quiet time
2:00 p.m.	Feed (breast or bottle): open room play time
6:00 p.m.	Feed (breast or bottle)*
10:00 p.m.	Feed (breast or bottle): check baby and put to bed for the night

* Many moms recommend keeping baby awake as much as possible during this time to help him sleep well during the night.

Three Months

Introduce solids at 10:00 a.m., 2:00 a.m., and 6:00 p.m.

6:00 a.m	Feed
9:30 a.m.	Bathe
10:00 a.m.	Feed: nap
2:00 p.m.	Feed: playtime
6:00 p.m.	Feed: put to bed
10:00 p.m.	Feed: put to bed for the night

Four Months

Continue with milk and solids at all three meals.

 7:00 a.m.   Feed
 9:00 a.m.   Bathe: put down for three hour nap
12:30 p.m.   Feed: play time (no scheduled nap)
 6:00 p.m.   Feed: put to bed (should sleep until morning)

Five Months

Continue four month schedule
Add sips of water from a cup

Seven Months to Twenty-four Months

Continue four months schedule
Wean baby from breast or formula (no need to add any milk
   to diet)

Two Years and Forward

Continue three meals daily
No need for naps
Put to bed after supper

Sleep Disturbances

Sometimes a young child's sleep will be disturbed for no
apparent reason. He may wake repeatedly, cry out, or grit his teeth.
You need to look for the cause. Common ones are alkaline urine
(from drinking juice), pinworms (see pages 51–52), television, and
tossing him in the air.

Immunizations

Vaccinations are safe and vital to your child's health. They should be administered according to the following schedule:

5 months:	DPT, polio
6 months:	DPT, polio
7 months:	DPT, polio
15 months:	MMR

No additional vaccinations are necessary for a baby who doesn't go to day care. All babies should be examined for possible illness before having the vaccinations. Don't have a sick baby vaccinated. Vaccinations should be administered in the deltoid muscle of the arm. Massage the area well after administering.

The first shots shouldn't be given before five months because the baby's immune system hasn't developed enough to respond effectively. After the initial DPT's, he won't need a tetanus shot for ten years unless he receives a wound in a horse lot or from a gunshot or a rusty nail. For safety sake, you may want to repeat the booster every ten years (see Vaccinations, Chapter Thirteen).

Occasionally a baby will develop fever from the vaccinations. It may begin four hours after the vaccination and last up to twenty four hours. Aspirin can be used to reduce the fever and help baby feel more comfortable (for dosages see pages 101–102). Dr. Denmark does not believe aspirin causes Reye's syndrome (see Reye's syndrome, pages 55, 78).

Note: If an unvaccinated child contracts whooping cough and survives the disease without medication, he is immune for life. If he is cured with antibiotics he is not immune and will need to be vaccinated to prevent further occurrence. Whooping cough is a serious illness and should always be treated with Erythromycin (see Whooping Cough, pages 85–86, 190–193; Erythromycin pages 91–92).

We treat babies more like toys, but they're human beings. A cow wouldn't do that to her calf!

When you bring a baby into the world, he is your responsibility. That child's not supposed to make you feel big; you're supposed to make him feel big. You need to give that child a chance.

I had a preacher's wife in my office one day. Her baby looked like the wrath of God. She said, "I want you to understand one thing, Dr. Denmark. My husband is a minister. I'm called to do so many things; I don't have time for this baby."

"Maybe you'd better go upstairs and read my Bible," I said. "It doesn't read like that. Mine says, 'Start in Jerusalem and go to Judea.'" If you bear a child, there's no sacrifice too great for that baby.

Danger Signs Indicating Emergency

It's 2:30 a.m. A frantic young mother picks up the phone and dials, cuddling a four-month-old infant in her left arm. A sleepy voice answers.

"Dr. Denmark, this is Madia Bowman."

"Yes, I hope everything is all right at the Bowman house."

"I apologize for calling you at this hour, but I didn't know what to do. My baby has a fever of 100 rectally..."

One might guess that baby Malinda survived the night! Under Dr. Denmark's patient instruction, I eventually learned to distinguish a true emergency from an illness that can wait until morning for professional attention. Children are seldom sick at convenient times. It's usually after office hours that a fever rises or a stomachache becomes severe. The following guidelines can help you distinguish true emergencies.

Fever

If a child has a fever, check him for meningitis.

Procedure

1. Lay him on his back.

2. Put a hand under the back of his neck and bend his head forward gently, bringing the chin toward the chest. A fussy child may stiffen his neck to resist examination, so calm and distract him while you check.

If the neck is stiff and will not bend, take him to the hospital emergency room.

3. Lay the child on his back.

4. Lift his knee and try to raise the leg at a right angle from body.

If legs are very stiff, it also indicates an emergency. A bulging fontanel (soft spot) on a newborn may also indicate meningitis.

Stomach Pain

If a child has stomach pain, first determine whether he has swallowed anything unusual. If he has, call your local poison control center immediately and follow their instructions. If he hasn't swallowed anything requiring a medical emergency, check him for appendicitis.

Procedure

1. Lay the child on his back.
2. Distract him with a toy.
3. Press his stomach between the right hipbone and navel
4. If he experiences sharp pain, he'll react to pressure in an obvious way. Sharp pain in this region indicates acute appendicitis. **Take him immediately to the emergency room.**

Note: Don't ask the child if this or that hurts. Children will normally answer "yes" whether they feel pain or not. It's important to distract him while pressing his abdomen.

Other Signs

- seizure
- a lot of red blood from rectum
- severe respiratory difficulty
- cyanosis (turning purple or blue indicates heart problems)

Dr. Denmark recommends training in CPR techniques and relief of airway obstruction (choking). Contact your local hospital for classes offered in your community. Don't fail to call 911 if your child's life is in imminent danger. If necessary it's best to go directly to a hospital whose emergency room specializes in the care of children.

If a mother doesn't have a good idea about what's wrong with her child, she shouldn't mess around and wait until he's in bad trouble. Most any doctor can recognize an emergency. In an emergency you need to go directly to where they can handle it.

Common Ailments

"Ow, ow! Mommy, I have a terrible cut on my finger!"
"David, come here and let me see your hand. Where is it?"
"On this one. Ow, it hurts!"
"I don't see it."
"Well...maybe it's on the other hand."

Soothing small hurts, real or imaginary, is an ordinary part of a mother's day. Cuts, scrapes, burns, bee stings—the list seems endless. In my early days of mothering, I was dialing Dr. Denmark for all kinds of minor complaints. As my family grew, so did the frequency of the phone calls. It finally occurred to me that I was repeating the same questions.

Cataloging her recommended treatment has been helpful to me and a time-saver for Dr. Denmark.

Stomachache

First check the child for possible poisoning or appendicitis (see page 32). If that's ruled out, watch for other symptoms—gas, diarrhea, vomiting, fever. With diarrhea or vomiting, he may have an intestinal infection or salmonella (food poisoning). Enemas are highly effective in combating intestinal disorders (see chapter four). If the stomachache is accompanied by a fever, he may need antibiotics (see chapter seven). For intestinal gas, a dose of Milk of Magnesia followed by a drink of warm water may bring relief. If an adult is ill, it might be helpful to drink water as hot as people usually drink tea or coffee. Children will not want to drink it as hot as adults.

Dosage

> 6 months–6 years: 1 teaspoon
> 6 years–adult: 2 teaspoons

Should the pain continue, check periodically for appendicitis and consult a physician.

Stomachs are very sensitive and are designed by the Creator to vomit easily as a form of protection against poison and bacteria. If a child has frequent stomachaches, observe him carefully over a period of time. Investigate the kinds of food he eats, eating patterns, the time of day stomachaches occur, and the environment and emotional state of the child. Sometimes children complain of stomachaches in an effort to gain attention. You may have to play detective to discover the cause.

Emergency Situations Related to Stomach Pain: appendicitis (see page 32), severe pain accompanied by bloody stools and/or a lot of red blood from the anus.

Motion Sickness

Motion sickness is more common in some families than in others. The tendency depends on the structure of the inner ear. It may be treated with Dramamine.

Headaches

The cause of headaches can be difficult to determine. If they are frequent, take your child for a physical examination. If the exam doesn't pinpoint the cause, his case requires further study.

Menstruation, excitement, eye strain, allergies, and too much sodium are common causes for teenagers' headaches. Gatorade, potato chips, and other salty foods should be avoided, and an eye exam may be in order. A child learning to read could be straining his eyes by reading too long and might need glasses.

Migrane headaches seem to run in families and may be stimulated by allergies due to almost anything. Some children have migraines after smelling asphalt, some after eating an onion. The child should be studied to see if there is a pattern to the headaches. If they continue for no explained reason, extensive testing (MRT, CT scans) may be necessary to rule out the possibility of a tumor.

Treatment for common headache: aspirin and a drink of warm water (see Aspirin: Dosage, pages 101–102). Dr. Denmark does not believe aspirin causes Reye's syndrome (see Reye's syndrome, pages 54–55, 78).

If a young child complains of his eyes hurting, it may indicate that he has a headache.

Skin

Cuts

Wide or deep cuts need immediate stitching before infection sets in. Wash minor cuts with soap and warm water. Rinse thoroughly and cleanse with alcohol. Silvadene cream can be applied to prevent or treat infection. Do not use peroxide. If the cut is open, tape it closed securely with a bandage. Do not wet or otherwise disturb the taped cut for seven days.

Thoroughly cleansing wounds with an antiseptic is important to promote healing and prevent possible blood poisoning (septicemia).

Scrapes

Clean a scrape the same way you treat a cut. Apply no dressing and keep it as dry as possible.

A Hard-to-Heal Scrape

When my son David was five-years-old, he scraped the inside of his ankle. The abrasion wasn't large, but I soon discovered he constantly rubbed it with his shoe and knocked it open. If he didn't wear shoes, dirt got into the wound. If I put on a Band-Aid, it became moist and oozed (typical of scrapes).

After a week, the scrape began to look worse. The area around it was turning red, indicating infection. Out of desperation, I forbade him to go outside, hoping to keep the area clean. He promptly tripped over a toy and set it bleeding again. I cleaned him up, confined him to a chair and called Dr. Denmark. Following her instructions, I covered the scrape with a generous application of Silvadene and a gauze bandage adhesive taped to his ankle. I changed the bandage at least once a day or whenever it got dirty. It was quite a trick to give him a bath without wetting the ankle. The treatment worked wonders, and the scrape healed quickly. I was thankful I didn't have to straitjacket my bouncy five-year-old to enable his ankle to heal!

Severe Infection

Possible Symptoms

- a lot of redness around the wound
- fever
- a knot in the groin (leg or foot wound)

- a knot in the armpit (arm or hand wound)
- a red streak

Treatment

1. Apply Silvadene cream generously.
2. Cover with a gauze bandage.
3. Change the dressing daily.
4. Keep the wound from getting wet.
5. Give antibiotics to fight infection. Ampicillin or penicilin are good options (see Antiobiotics, Chapter Seven).
6. You may have to consult a doctor.

Burns

A third-degree burn (a deep, severe burn) needs to be treated immediately at the hospital. First-and second-degree burns can be dressed with Silvadene cream to prevent secondary infection and guard against scarring.

Treatment

1. Put Silvadene on gauze thickly.
2. Place dressing over burn.
3. Bind by wrapping with more gauze.
4. Leave dressing on for four days.
5. Redress after four days if necessary.
6. Keep the affected area dry.

Eczema

If a child's skin is scaly, often in patches, he may have eczema, which tends to break out where the most perspiration occurs. Eczema is an allergic reaction to some environmental factor. Any irritant can cause eczema if allergy is present. In addition to treating the condition, try to play "detective" and determine the cause of the allergy. Common offenders are food, soap, fabrics, and tobacco smoke. If your child is prone to eczema, carefully rinse away soap and shampoos when bathing him. If a baby has eczema, bathe him only once a week, rinsing thoroughly (see page 9). Avoid perfumed soaps and those that leave a residue. Ivory is often the best. Safeguard is another we Bowmans use with good results for our children who have particularly sensitive skin. Every individual's skin is different, so keep trying various soaps until you find one that seems to work well with your child's skin.

Treatment

If the eczema is merely scaly,
1. Wash skin with sterile water and dry.
2. Apply one 10th of 1% Kenalog cream twice a day.

If the eczema looks infected (like an ulcer),
1. Wash with sterile water and dry.
2. Apply Silvadene twice a day, alternating with the Kenalog cream. For example, Silvadene in the morning; Kenalog at noon; Silvadene in the evening, Kenalog at bedtime.

If the eczema involves a fungal infection (characterized by watery, scaly skin),
1. Apply Silvadene cream twice a day.
2. Shake Mycostatin powder on top of the Silvadene.

Rashes (General)

There are a host of reasons an individual breaks out in a rash. Generally speaking, but not always, the following principles apply: A systemic rash covers the entire body or is concentrated in areas of heavier perspiration such as the crook of the arms or back of the knees. It is a reaction to something the child has eaten or drunk. A rash which covers only parts of the body and isn't concentrated in those areas is a reaction to something contacted by the skin such as new-fabric dye, poison ivy, soaps. With any severe rash or one associated with a fever, call your physician.

Poison Ivy or Poison Oak

The rash is characterized by redness and blisters and is caused by contact with the oil from the plant. It will last fourteen days from the time of contact.

Treatment

1. Keep the affected area completely dry to prevent infection.
2. Chlor-Trimeton or Benadryl syrup will reduce itching (for dosages see pages 102–103).
3. Caladryl or witch hazel applied locally also reduces itching.

If your child has previously exhibited a sensitivity to poison ivy and has recently been exposed, the following procedure removes the oil and may minimize allergic reaction. It must be done before redness and swelling develop.

1. Rub the exposed skin at once with Clorox.
2. Rinse with water immediately.

If the skin becomes infected, further treatment is necessary. Silvadene cream may be applied.

Jellyfish stings can be treated in the same way.

Athlete's Foot

Athlete's foot is a fungal infection characterized by an itchy rash on the soles of the feet and betwen the toes. It can cause the skin to crack and peel.

Make sure your child's feet stay clean, dry and that he wears cotton socks with his tennis shoes. Apply Mycostatin powder twice a day until it goes away.

Ringworm

Ringworm is not caused by a worm but is a fungal infection most often found on children who lack a balanced diet. It is a round, itchy rash with a red-edged ring which temporarily destroys the hair on location. The rash usually consists of one or two patches the size of a quarter or larger. These can occur anywhere on the body.

Ringworm should be treated with an antifungal medication such as Mycostatin powder twice a day until it disappears. Examine the child's diet to see if there is a deficiency, especially in Vitamin B (see Chapter Eleven).

Impetigo

Impetigo is a staph infection of the skin. It usually looks like a burn and may have a greenish color. It can develop from anything that causes a break in the skin—a bite, burn, sunburn, nettle, or cut. The skin peels.

Treatment

1. Soak off the scabs gently in warm water.
2. Wash the area well with soap and water. Be sure to rinse off all the soap, and don't make the area bleed.
3. Dab on Silvadene cream.

The procedure may need to be repeated twice a day for up to one week.

Sunburn

A child needs a moderate amount of sunshine for good health. The vitamin D obtained from the sun is vital, but don't allow him to bake in the sun. The use of sunscreens is also questionable. It's best to cover the skin with clothing. If he plays a long time in the sun he needs a hat to guard against sunstroke as well as sunburn. A kimono is ideal for babies playing in the sand.

Treatment

Sunburn should be treated like any other bad burn. Silvadene cream may be applied (see Burns, page 39).

Boils

With a true abscess, there is a white blister on top.

Treatment

1. Clean with alcohol.
2. Use sterilized needle to open boil.
3. Pull skin away from center to drain (don't mash in).
4. After draining, dress with Silvadene cream.

Hot applications or soaking boils in warm water will make them feel better. If there is a great deal of heat or redness around the boil and/or a red streak appears, seek professional help at once.

Acne

If your teenager has acne, look for an allergy. The most common allergies are to milk products, citrus fruits, and chocolate.

Treatment

Wash the skin well with soap and water in the evening, rinsing thoroughly. In the morning, wipe the oiliest part of the child's face with alcohol and rinse with cold water. Make sure he is eating a proper diet (see Chapter Eleven).

Chapped Skin

As soon as the weather turns chilly, my children get chapped hands and faces. The skin on the backs of the boys' hands begin to resemble sandpaper.

Dr. Denmark recommends a very light layer of Vaseline applied to chapped skin twice a day. Instruct your child to rinse soap thoroughly and carefully dry his hands. Discourage him from licking his lips.

Bites and Stings

Bee, wasp, fire ant

Treatment

1. Promptly apply Clorox. Must apply before swelling and redness occur.
2. Wash off immediately with water.
3. Apply witch hazel or alcohol.
4. Give dose of Chlor-Trimeton or Benadryl syrup every eight hours if needed (dosage indicated below).
5. Can apply caladryl ointment to reduce itching.

Chlor-Trimeton or Benadryl Dosage

0–6 months:	1/2 teaspoon syrup or a crushed quarter tablet (see page 103)
6 months–adult:	1 teaspoon syrup or a crushed half tablet (see page 103)

For any severe allergic reaction evidenced by breathing difficulties or welts covering the body take the child to the emergency room.

Ticks

Treatment

1. Apply gasoline to the tick with a Q-Tip. Be careful not to touch the surrounding skin. Kerosene and Raid are also effective.
2. After one minute, pull the tick off with tweezers. Be careful to remove the entire tick, including the head.
3. Wash well with soap and water.
4. Apply Mercurochrome or alcohol to cleanse the area.

Mosquito and Other Common Insect Bites

Treatment

Wipe bites with alcohol or Mercurochrome. If an allergic reaction occurs, resulting in large welts, give the child Chlor-Trimeton or Benadryl syrup in the same dosage as for bee stings. Itching can be treated with Caladryl ointment or witch hazel.

Scratched bites can become infected with impetigo and begin to ooze. If this happens, treat with Silvadene cream twice a day. Any bites that blister should be cleansed with alcohol or Mechrochrome.

Minor Dog and Cat Bites

Treatment

Cleanse the wound thoroughly with soap and water, then alcohol. Leave it open to the air. Study the animal to be sure its behavior is not abnormal. Observe it for possible illness. Inquire as to whether it has received its shots. If the animal is ill, call a physician and animal control immediately. If your child has been bitten and you cannot find the animal, consult a physician immediately.

Cat-scratch Fever

Cat-scratch fever is relatively rare; but if your child is scratched and develops a swollen lymph node and/or abcesses, he may have contracted it. Consult a physician. Penicillin is effective (see Antibiotics, Chapter Seven). Thorough cleansing of scratches helps prevent this kind of infection.

Venomous Snake Bites

Treatment

Give the child two teaspoons of Benadryl or Chlor-Trimeton syrup (one 4mg tablet), put ice directly on the puncture wounds, and go immediately to the hospital emergency room.

Lice

Lice are recognized by severe itching and small white specks attached to the hair that cannot be easily removed. The specks (eggs) are usually around the ears. Use Kwell and follow the directions on the box. Special fine-tooth combs help remove the eggs and can be found at most pharmacies.

Swallowing Objects

If a child swallows a medium-sized object such as a marble, coin, or pin, look for it in his stools for up to ten days. If the object is not passed or he is experiencing pain, consult a physician. An X-ray may be necessary.

Blow to the Head

Elevate the head and try to keep the child as quiet as possible to minimize internal bleeding. I have used suckers to console a child who received one. Vomiting is common with head injuries and may not be a danger sign. Apply ice to the bump if it doesn't make the child cry.

Look for danger signs—eyes not focusing, unequal dilation in the eyes, poor sense of balance, or other abnormal behavior. Shining a flashlight in the child's eyes and observing the response of his pupils will help detect unequal dilation. If such signs are present, go to the hospital emergency room.

A blow to the side of the head is potentially more dangerous than on the front or back because the skull is thinner there. Heavier bones over the eyes and at the back protect the brain better.

Conjunctivitis

Conjunctivitis is caused by clogged tear ducts, often induced by allergies and colds. Pus develops in the eyes when they get stopped up. If not treated they may become red and infected. Many call this condition "pinkeye," although it is not true "pinkeye."

Treatment

Opening tear duct:
1. Place a small piece of sterile cotton on your index finger.
2. Put your finger under the child's eye. Gently press the corner next to the nose and pull down.
3. Repeat the procedure four times daily.

Warm compresses:
1. Take a warm wet washcloth or ball of cotton and squeeze it out, placing it over the eye for a few minutes.
2. When the compress cools, dip it in warm water and repeat the procedure.
3. Soak the eye in this manner four times daily.

If the eye does not respond to the treatment after a few days or the eyeball becomes red, see a doctor.

Dr. Denmark has used Argyrol for years to treat eye infections (see page 105). She puts one drop in each eye daily for three days (never longer).

Occasionally a child is born with a closed tear duct that must be opened surgically. It may be indicated if the eye continues to secrete pus following full treatment.

Fainting

Treatment

Turn the child on his stomach and wait for him to revive. If he doesn't revive immediately, hold some ammonia under his nose for a few seconds and cover his face with a cold cloth. If this procedure does not revive him, go immediately to the emergency room. In any case consult a physician to determine the cause for his fainting.

Menstrual Pain

Menstrual pain is caused by the tightening of the cervical muscle during menses.

Anything which makes a young girl tense can aggravate menstrual pain. Encourage her to relax so blood can flow easily through the cervix.

Treatment

1. Avoid all caffeine.
2. Drink a glass of hot water and take an aspirin.
3. Stretch out on the bed on her stomach and rest.

Minor Mouth Sores

If a child gets mouth sores frequently, study his diet for a possible deficiency that would lower the body's resistance. Lack of vitamin B is a common one.

Treatment

Paint the sores with a little Mercurochrome on the end of a Q-Tip once a day for three days. Gargling with Listerine or salt water may be helpful. The salt content should be no more than 1 teaspoon per quart of water. A higher concentration may irritate the tissues of the mouth and throat.

Swimmer's Ear

Putting one's head under water can cause infection. If your child complains of an earache after swimming, press the V-shaped protrusion on the outside part of his ear above the earlobe next to his cheek. If the pressure is painful, he may have swimmer's ear. An abscessed ear does not hurt more when pressed (see pages 81–83). Swimmer's ear is a fungus infection and will need eardrops prescribed by a physician. Use until the pain goes away.

A few drops of rubbing alcohol in the ear canal right after swimming will help remove the water that promotes the infection.

Swimming pools are about the dirtiest things we have created. There are urine and feces in pools. They're filthy...but it is important for children to learn to swim.

Our ears are similar to those of a dog, cat, or horse. You never see any of them put their heads under water when they're swimming. They have too much sense.

I was born and reared near Savannah, Georgia; but we lived on a farm so I never learned to swim as a child. As an adult I had nightmares about kids drowning. The dreams repeated the same scenario—there were children stranded on a sand bar. The tide was coming in, and I was helpless to do anything.

At age sixty-one I became determined to learn to swim. We were traveling on a ship at the time, and there was a pool available to the passengers. I borrowed Mary's bathing suit (Eustace thought I had lost my mind), got up early to avoid being seen, and began to teach myself. There were a few kids up at that early hour, and they tried to coach me. "Dr. Denmark, if you don't put your head under the water, you'll never learn to swim," they'd say.

"Never will my head get wet," I told them. Ten days later, oof, oof, I was going the length of the pool! My head never went under, but I learned to swim and the nightmares stopped.

Nosebleeds

Nosebleeds occur when the septum vessels are broken. They are close to the surface and rupture if the nose is twisted or bumped.

Nosebleeds are more common in some families than others.

Treatment

1. Have the child stand up straight. Don't lift his chin.
2. Put pressure under the child's nose by pressing down on the upper lip, and put ice on the nose.
3. In a few minutes a clot will have formed, and the bleeding stops. The clot can then be gently blown out. If nosebleeds occur frequently the nose may have to be cauterized. If they still continue, the child's blood should be studied for possible leukemia, rheumatic fever, or diabetes.

Pinworms

Pinworms are everywhere. A child can contract them by eating with unwashed hands, biting nails, sucking fingers, and eating mucous from his nose. Symptoms are restless sleep, gritting teeth, and crying out while sleeping. Observe the child's anus with a flashlight at night in the dark. The white, thin worms are often evident. They are twice as long as an eyelash and pointed on the ends.

Treatment

1 One Vermox tablet a day for three days. Dosage is the same for all ages.*
2. Disinfect door knobs and toilet handles by wiping them with rubbing alcohol.

* Many physicians prescribe one tablet, one time for pinworms. Others prescribe two dosages a week apart. Dr. Denmark, however, believes the above treatment to be most effective.

A child can get pinworms repeatedly as long as he puts his hands in his mouth. Treat him each time, but he should not have Vermox more frequently than every three months.

Sties

A sty is a small boil formed on the rim of an eyelid.

Treatment

Apply warm compresses two or three times daily. After the boil begins to drain on its own, apply Silvadene cream twice a day until complete healing takes place.

Digestive Disorders and Enemas

It was a beautiful morning, and things were running smoothly for the Bowman household. The older children were seated at the breakfast table. Baby David was gobbling down a huge bowl of mush. I had just wiped his hands and face when his entire breakfast came up all over the highchair tray.

He couldn't be sick, I thought. He must have just gagged. I'll watch him and see. When the mess was cleaned up, I placed another bowl of mush on the tray and began spooning it into his mouth. Suddenly, I heard telltale noises from three-year-old Esther. She had vomited on the table and the floor as well.

With a sense of desperation, I grabbed a rag and several towels. The telephone rang. After hoisting a crying baby David onto my hip, I answered—wrong number. No sooner had I put down the phone when David threw up his second breakfast onto my shoulder. A minute later, Esther was sick again, this time on the living room couch.

I made a beeline for the Milk of Magnesia and took the enema bag out of the closet. Whew! What a way to start the day!

Diagnosing Digestive Disorders

Dr. Denmark recommends milk of magnesia for a variety of intestinal ailments. Its laxative effect helps the digestive tract recover.

When a child has stomach pain he should first be checked for possible poisoning or appendicitis (see page 32). If the stomach pain is mild, a dose of milk of magnesia may be all he needs (see pages 35–36).

On Dr. Denmark's recommended diet, constipation shouldn't be a problem, but if it occurs, milk of magnesia is again recommended. When a child's stools are slightly abnormal (unusual consistency and strong odor) or he has mild diarrhea, give him milk of magnesia and watch for other symptoms. A fever may indicate the need for an antibiotic (see page 61). With vomiting and persistent diarrhea, enemas are probably in order.

Purpose of Enemas

Vomiting and diarrhea are immediate signals that the body is trying to cleanse itself of bacteria or food poisoning. Giving medication merely to stop the symptoms is not a wise method of treating intestinal disorders. The foreign matter needs to be expelled to enable the body to recover quickly.

In most cases enemas are particularly effective in treating digestive disorders. They help stop vomiting and diarrhea, prevent dehydration, and are an effective guard against **Reye's syndrome**. Reye's syndrome is caused by vomiting and diarrhea after which the blood becomes so thick it clots (vascular coagulation). Enemas can prevent thickening of the blood. If a child cannot keep down fluid and has diarrhea, enemas prevent dehydration because fluid is absorbed through the colon. The chemical makeup of Dr. Denmark's enemas soothes the stomach and restores the balance of electrolytes. Enemas can also help bring down a high fever by replenishing vital body fluids.

I frequently saw Reye's syndrome when I worked in the slums. Children would come in so dehydrated they looked like mummies. I remember one particular case when I was interning at Egelston Hospital. Dr. Hoppy said to me, "Dr. Denmark, there's no point in trying to treat that child. It's simply too late." I put a needle in the child's arm and pumped in 50 ccs of 50 percent glucose. The baby was playing in a few minutes. He wasn't dehydrated anymore. The first thing a doctor will do for a person with Reye's syndrome is to put him on IV's in an effort to dilute the blood and keep it from clotting. If the blood clots, the patient will die or become brain damaged (see Reye's syndrome, page 78).

Standard Enema

Method
1. Purchase Enema bag kit from pharmacy (see page 103).
2. Give child Milk of Magnesia (dosage indicated below).
3. Wait two hours.
4. Administer standard enema.

Milk of Magnesia Dosage
0–6 months:	1/2 teaspoon
6 months–6 years:	1 teaspoon
6 years–adult:	2 teaspoons

If the child vomits the Milk of Magnesia within ten minutes, repeat the dose once and then leave him alone. The standard enema consists of boiled water cooled to body temperature and mixed with baking soda.

Measurements

         0–1 year: 1/4 teaspoon baking soda and 8 oz. water
  1 year–6 years: 1 teaspoon baking soda and 1 pint water
  6 years–adult: 2 teaspoons baking soda and quart of water

Procedure

1. Hang solution-filled enema bag.
2. Expel air from tube by letting a little water flow from nozzle. Pinch off tube quickly to prevent wasting the rest of the solution.
3. Put Vaseline on appropriate size nozzle.
4. Lay child over lap and carefully insert nozzle 1–1 1/2 inches into rectum, with tip pointing toward his navel.
5. Hold buttocks and let water go in slowly.
6. It's best not to let the solution be expelled for ten minutes. Hold the baby's buttocks together to prevent early expulsion.

The sooner the enema is administered, the more effective it is in cleansing the digestive tract of offending food or bacteria because there has been less time for absorption. Start with the Milk of Magnesia right after your child first vomits, and two hours later administer the enema. Don't wait for repeated vomiting. Occasionally a hard stool will block fluid. Administer the enema gently without forcing. Sliding nozzle slightly in and out of the rectum will better allow water to flow.

With excessive vomiting and diarrhea the body may absorb most or all of the enema instead of discharging it. Absorption prevents dehydration. When a child is given an enema, he may expel the solution up to twelve hours later in the form of watery stools. If he is still having frequent, watery stools after twelve hours, they should be attributed to diarrhea, not the enema.

Retention Enema (Tea Enema)

If the child continues to vomit and cannot retain fluids after you have given a standard enema, a retention enema may be indicated to prevent dehydration and restore the balance of electrolytes.

Procedure

1. Put 1 teabag in 10 oz. water. Boil 3 minutes. Stir the tea bag around in the water and remove.
2. Mix the following:

- 8 oz. tea solution
- 24 oz. boiled water
- 1/2 teaspoon baking soda
- 1/2 teaspoon salt
- 2 tablespoons dextrose or white Karo syrup.

3. Warm the above mixture to body temperature and give 8 oz. as an enema every two hours for four doses. For example:

- 8 oz. at 10:00 a.m.
- 8 oz. at 12:00 noon
- 8 oz. at 2:00 p.m.
- 8 oz. at 4:00 p.m.

All ages have the same dosage—even infants. It's best if the enema solutions are retained for ten minutes before expulsion.

There is no question in my mind that enemas have saved us at least half a dozen trips to the emergency room. Several of my children seem to have particularly sensitive stomachs. When they start vomiting nothing stays down. It can be pretty dangerous and scary, especially with an infant. With severe vomiting, I resort to the retention enema and it works wonders. Usually by the second dose, vomiting has stopped.

Some doctors would lose their false teeth if they heard my advice about enemas—but enemas certainly do work!

One doctor told me, "Enemas went out with the Greeks!" Not so. My patients use them with great success. And I've never had a child develop Reye's syndrome who was treated with enemas.

Further Information on Preventing Dehydration

Dehydration is of concern when a child cannot retain fluids over an extended period of time because of severe vomiting and/or diarrhea. It can be life threatening. Symptoms are sunken eyes, rapid heart beat, lack of urination, and general weakness.

If your child is thirsty, give him water even if he vomits it up. His body will absorb some of it. Make sure the water is warm. Pedialyte can be given along with the enema to restore the electrolyte balance in a child who has had digestive problems. It is helpful for any age.

If you are concerned that your infant is becoming dehydrated, give him an enema and offer him frequent drinks of Pedialyte and warm water. Don't nurse or bottle feed more frequently than the recommended schedule (see pages 27–28). Increasing the frequency of "milk meals" may further irritate his stomach and be counterproductive.

A Lesson Learned

Our Leila was eighteen months old when the following incident occurred. She had been very chipper, but her bowels were not normal. We had changed one or two bad diapers a day for close to a week. Her stools were of abnormal consistency with an unusually strong odor. She had no fever or vomiting, so I merely gave her some Milk of Magnesia and watched her behavior.

Suddenly Leila's appetite dropped, but there was still no other symptoms. We speculated that the muggy weather might be affecting her.

For two days she ate very little, and I was becoming concerned. The evening of the second day I again dosed her with a little Milk of Magnesia and put her to bed. My plan was to give her an enema in the morning and call Dr. Denmark if her appetite didn't improve. That night she seemed restless and weak. I chided myself for being overly concerned. Surely she was just tired. I was pushing the alarm button for no good reason. Hadn't I done that numerous times in the past?

At 5:00 a.m. I awoke and checked her. To my dismay, I found her so weak she could hardly sit. I immediately called Dr. Denmark. She asked me some questions, and I checked Leila's pulse rate. Dr. Denmark concluded that our baby had been fighting a relatively mild intestinal infection but was in serious condition because of dehydration.

I quickly gave Leila a retention enema and frequent sips of Pedialyte or warm water to restore her electrolyte balance and fluids. She regained strength and later her appetite.

In retrospect I was baffled. How in the world had she become dehydrated? I had always been so careful to watch my babies' fluid intake and retention, especially if they were vomiting or had severe diarrhea. But Leila had neither, and I was caught off guard.

Somehow we had been so focused on her not eating that we failed to note her lack of fluid intake. At eighteen months most of her water came from pureed foods, and babies who aren't eating can become dehydrated rather quickly. The moral of this story is: carefully monitor your baby's fluid intake and retention, especially if he isn't feeling well.

Recovery Diet

After a digestive disorder take special care not to give a child food that will irritate his stomach. If vomiting has been severe, it may take extra time to adjust to a normal diet. Begin by trying sips of the following:

- warm tea or water
- peppermint drops
- pear juice
- broth (either chicken or beef are fine)
- thin rice cereal

As he begins to recover, these foods are appropriately mild:

- bananas
- applesauce
- lean beef
- chicken
- rice
- toast without butter
- baked potatoes without butter

Avoid all milk products and fatty foods.

Antibiotics and Intestinal Disorders

If a child is running a fever with an intestinal problem, he may need antibiotics after the vomiting has stopped (see Chapter Seven).

For persistent diarrhea but no fever or vomiting, first try an enema. Should it continue, the next step is to determine whether the problem is food related. There may be an intestinal infection, even without fever. Erythromycin is an effective antibiotic for intestinal infections (see pages 91–92). If the diarrhea is not at all affected by the antibiotic, the child may need testing at a hospital.

Note: For information on preventing infectious intestinal disorders, see How to Stop Passing the "Bugs" Around, pages 86–87.

Fever

sther's rectal temperature was 105.5°. I stared at the thermometer in disbelief. What if it kept rising? What if she didn't recover? Panic rose in my chest as I looked at my little daughter lying listlessly on the couch. Her complexion was pale, the usual cheery smile had disappeared, and her normally sparkling eyes were dull and glassy. Oh, how I wanted my bouncy Esther back again! After five anxious days her temperature dropped, and as Dr. Denmark predicted, she broke out in a rash typical of German measles.

Fever can be frightening. High temperatures are also a blessing, however. They are the body's alarm system, alerting us to sickness. There is hardly a child who never experiences a fever. Every mother needs to know how to diagnose and treat it.

Diagnosing a Fever

When a child is uncharacteristically fussy and warm to the touch, take his temperature. A glass thermometer is recommended (oral or rectal).

Procedure

Rectal (infants and toddlers)
1. Shake the mercury down.
2. Lay baby over your lap and gently insert the thermometer one inch.
3. Pinch buttocks gently around the thermometer to keep it in place and hold for one or two minutes before reading.

Underarm (young children)
1. Shake the mercury down.
2. Place the bulb of the thermometer in the child's armpit.
3. Bring the arm down over the end of the thermometer and hold securely for two or three minutes. Try to keep the armpit airtight.

Oral (for older children who will not bite the thermometer or break it)
1. Shake the mercury down.
2. Place the bulb of the thermometer under the tongue and instruct the child to keep it there with his mouth closed for one to two minutes.

One degree above the following readings indicates a fever: under arm (97), oral (98.6), rectal (99.6).

Fever is caused by infection. Scientists aren't certain what it does but have observed that different germs cause fever with varying characteristics. With a strep infection, the temperature typically runs low in the morning and may even be subnormal before noon. Then it usually begins to rise, peaks at 6:00 p.m., and goes down around 2:00 a.m.

Fevers accompanying flu or German measles tend to remain fairly consistent throughout the day. A fever brought on by an abscess usually drops when the abscess is opened.

Treatment

If your child registers an abnormal temperature, first check him for meningitis (pages 31–32). Meningitis is always an emergency. If the fever's cause is not evident, periodically check for its symptoms. If any are present, go immediately to the hospital. When meningitis is ruled out, look for the following:
- a cold (pages 71–73)
- swollen glands in neck under jaws (pages 78–79)
- a throat redder than the color of his gums (pages 78–79)
- pulling at ears (pages 81–83)
- stomachache (pages 35–36)
- diarrhea (see Chapter Four)
- vomiting (see Chapter Four)

If an intestinal disturbance is evident, an enema is probably in order (see Chapter Four). If symptoms are mild, inconclusive, and/or indicate an upper respiratory problem, the following are recommended:

1. A hot bath. Run the shower first so the room will be warm and steamy. Dry him off and put on pajamas from another room.
2. Aspirin (dosage indicated below)
3. Bundle the child up. When he starts to perspire, usually around the back of the neck, begin taking layers off. Change wet clothing.
4. Continue to observe the child for a rising temperature and other symptoms.

Aspirin Dosage*

1–3 months:	Mix 1 crushed baby aspirin and 5 teaspoons water; give 1 teaspoon.
3–5 months:	Mix 1 crushed baby aspirin and 4 teaspoons water; give 1 teaspoon.
5–7 months:	Mix 1 crushed baby aspirin and 3 teaspoons water; give 1 teaspoon.
7–12 months:	Mix 1 crushed baby aspirin and 2 teaspoons water; give 1 teaspoon.
12 months:	One whole baby aspirin. If he won't swallow a tablet, crush it and mix it with water or honey.
12 months–adult:	Consult bottle for dosage.

* Repeat every four hours as needed.

Dr. Denmark is certain that aspirin does not cause Reye's syndrome (see pages 54–55, 78).

With a high fever a child has chills. Many infants and toddlers will sit in their mothers' laps and want to be cuddled for warmth. Applying cool cloths to the child's forehead or cool baths is not recommended. Cold baths may cause a seizure.

Boy, I'm going to meet "they" someday and really get educated. A woman called the other day with a baby who had a fever. "Give the baby a little aspirin," I said.

"They say you shouldn't give a baby aspirin," the mother said.

I said, "Then why'd you bother me? Do what 'they' say. If 'they' know what to do, why bother Dr. Denmark and waste her time?"

Fever and Enemas

A fever may inhibit digestion and thereby cause vomiting and diarrhea. Enemas will help. They can actually help reduce any high fever by replenishing vital body fluids. Sometimes aspirin may be added to the enema if the child cannot keep it down orally (see Chapter Four).

Diagnosing the Severity of an Illness

Every child's reaction to infection is individual. Some typically run higher temperatures than others. One may have a low fever and be very sick, though another's temperatures may spike with the least illness. Some have a tendency to complain intensely with the least illness, while others hardly complain at all, even when they are very sick. Our Leila can spike 105 degrees and still be coherent, while Steven has been delirious at 101 degrees.

You need to evaluate the child's general behavior to determine the severity of the ailment. Observe his appetite, playfulness, and coordination in addition to his temperature and compare his behavior to what it normally is.

Your instincts are often accurate. If you're worried and not sure what the problem is, consult a physician. Any high or prolonged fever may indicate a need for antibiotics (see Antibiotics, Chapter Seven).

Lots of kids get "busitis." They wake up in the morning desperately ill. As soon as the school bus leaves, there's an amazing recovery!

Recovery

It's easy to assume a child is well when his temperature is down in the morning. However, temperatures due to staph and strep infections characteristically drop in the morning even before true recovery. Just because he appears well, don't send him back to school or take him to church. Going into public too soon may prolong illness and infect other children. The child's white blood cell count may be low, rendering him more susceptible to picking up something else. He should have at least two fever-free evenings before resuming his normal routine.

Infectious  Diseases

Steven announced dramatically, "I'm sick and need to see Dr. Denmark." He trudged into the living room toting his plastic doctor's kit. I was clearing the lunch dishes. Out of the corner of my eye I saw him fluff a pillow on the couch, climb aboard, and pull a blanket up to his chin.

Methodically, he felt his forehead and stuck the toy thermometer in his mouth. When the kitchen was clean twenty minutes later, I brought a basket of laundry into the living room to fold. He was still lying on the couch with the toy thermometer protruding from his mouth.

"Are you still playing doctor?"

"I have a throat infection," came the muffled reply, teeth clenched around the thermometer.

"You poor baby," I crooned. I walked to the couch and laid a kiss on his forehead. It was warm. I felt his neck.

"Steven," I remarked in surprise, "You do have a sore throat." His brown eyes looked puzzled.

"I told you I was sick."

Our children are generally very healthy, but we aren't exempt from colds, sore throats, and the like, especially during winter months.

Common illnesses can become serious if not treated properly. With Dr. Denmark's help I am learning to diagnose and treat them.

Today young pediatricians tend to avoid treating their patients until an illness is severe. That's not my way. In my opinion, if a physician sees something wrong, he ought to take care of the problem before it becomes severe.

Aspirin is recommended throughout this chapter to combat fever and aches (see Dosages, pages 101–102). Dr. Denmark is certain that aspirin does not cause Reye's syndrome (see pages 54–55, 78).

Diagnosis of Common Illnesses

Carefully observe your child's behavior and apparent physical condition. Look for specific symptoms to indicate the problem.

- fever
- a throat redder than his gums
- swollen neck glands
- congestion
- runny nose
- coughing
- pulling at ears
- stomach ache
- abnormal stools with an unusually strong odor
- diarrhea
- vomiting
- rashes

- loss of appetite
- head ache
- inconsolable crying
- burning sensation when urinating
- lethargy and weakness
- unusual crankiness

Normally symptoms will indicate one particular illness, but occasionally a child may be fighting more than one at a time. For example, he may have flu and chicken pox, food poisoning and an infected ear. Both must be treated at the same time. Dr. Denmark prefers broadbased antibiotics and these are effective in treating a variety of illnesses simultaneously. Also, her schedule for administering antibiotics should be carefully followed (see Chapter Seven).

Symptoms may be inconclusive. If there is no emergency (see Chapter Two), you may have to wait a few hours until more definitive indications surface.

Years ago when I first started practicing medicine, if a doctor didn't know what was wrong he would say the patient was bilious. Biliousness wore out. Now doctors just say its a virus. Now everything is a virus.

Colds

A child with a cold needs care to prevent secondary infections of sinus, ear, and throat. Keep him warm, give him plenty of fluids, feed him well, and help him rest. Aspirin will make him feel better and reduce inflammation. If he's very congested, clean out his nose so he can breathe better.

Procedure

1. Twist a piece of sterile cotton onto the end of a Q-Tip so that it hangs approximately an inch off the end of the stick.
2. Dip the end of the cotton into Argyrol or saline solution (1 tsp. salt per quart of water) and squeeze off excess.
3. Twist the end of the cotton into the child's nostril (only the cotton should enter the nostril) and pull it out. Repeat for other side. Use the procedure once daily for no longer than three days.

Argyrol is presently unavailable on the market, so Dr. Denmark recommends using the saline solution indicated above.

Sitting in a steamy bathroom can also relieve congestion. Close the door, turn the shower on hot, and stay with the child until he is breathing more easily. Dry him off and dress him in clothes from another room.

Don't use a vaporizer. Vaporizers or humidifiers increase the moisture in the house and encourage the growth of mold, a common allergen. If necessary, use a dehumidifier.

I'll tell you how those cold-air vaporizers got started. Years ago mothers noticed that if their babies had the croup, rocking them on the porch helped. No, it wasn't the cold air that enabled them to breathe better—it was the clean air. Everyone inside was smoking.

Once I was notified that a patient in the hospital with croup was desperately ill. When I arrived, I found they had put the child in a tent, breathing ice cold mist.

"Take that baby out of there," I said to the nurse. Bring me a rocking chair and a blanket. Let mama roll him in it up good and tight and rock him for a while. Within a few minutes the child was much better. There's no excuse for a cold air vaporizer. Nobody in his right mind would go to a cold, wet climate to get well.

Never use a suction device in the nose. If your child's nose is running clear, it probably indicates an allergy (see Chapter Eight). If the discharge is not clear, he has a sinus infection. A fever with the cold may indicate a secondary infection. If he has a fever in the morning, give him a hot bath and aspirin and observe him. Should his condition worsen by afternoon, you may want to see a physician and use antibiotics.

With any excessive or persistent fever, notify a physician.

Coughing

Never use cough medicine. When the cough reflex is suppressed the lungs can fill with fluid, and pneumonia may develop. Coughing, sneezing, and runny noses are nature's way of cleaning out the system. An expectorant or decongestant should not be used either.

Coughs often get worse at night or early in the morning when the child first wakes up, often due to postnasal drainage.

If a minor but persistent cough keeps him awake, try giving him something sweet. A little honey, sugar, Karo syrup, or a peppermint drop might help. (Exercise discernment concerning the age of your child before giving him a peppermint. A young child risks inhaling it.) The sugar makes saliva flow and dilutes the mucus which may be causing the cough.

Aspirin is also effective in treating a minor cough caused by postnasal drainage. It helps dry up the drainage and reduces swelling in the nasal passages. Chlor-Trimeton or Benadryl syrup may also be used to treat this type of cough (dosage indicated below).

With excessive, deep coughing, the child should see a physician (see Whooping Cough, pages 85–86).

Chlor-Trimeton or Benadryl Dosage

0–6 months:	1/2 teaspoon syrup or a crushed quarter tablet (see page 103)
6 months–adult:	1 teaspoon syrup or a crushed half tablet (see page 103)

Even if a baby's coughing at night bothers you, never give him cough syrup. No, no! If it bothers you so much, maybe you parents should consider taking something to get to sleep!

Wheezing

Wheezing when breathing *in* indicates croup. Take the child into a steamy bathroom. Give him a hot bath and aspirin. An antibiotic may be needed with fever (see Antiobiotics, Chapter Seven).

Wheezing when breathing *out* indicates asthma. It is produced by allergens and the cause(s) should always be investigated (see Allergies, Chapter Eight). Give the child aspirin, warm or hot water to drink, and an antibiotic if there is fever. Do not use a vaporizer.

Flu

Symptoms are headache, fever, and chills. Fever can prevent proper digestion of food, so the child may also suffer intestinal distress. Be sure he stays warm and well hydrated. Encourage him to rest and keep him at home, isolated from other germs. Aspirin may be used for fever and enemas are useful in combating vomiting and diarrhea. Flu takes the following course:

Day One: The child is miserable with fever, chills, headache, and possibly digestive disorders.

Day Two: Feels better.

Day Three: Feels considerably better and will often want to resume a normal schedule. Unfortunately, it is on the third day that the white blood cell count drops drastically. At this time resistance to secondary infections is almost nil. Before antibiotics were discovered, death was not uncommon from secondary infections contracted in the aftermath of flu. He should be pampered for a week after symptoms have subsided to allow time for his resistance to build again.

Antibiotics are often needed to prevent secondary infections. Ampicillin is recommended.

There is no effective immunization against flu simply because one can catch it repeatedly. Immunizations only work against diseases like whooping cough that give lifetime immunity.

Chicken Pox

Chicken pox begins as a red rash, round and flat, that develops into elevated bumps with clear blisters on top. There may also be swollen lymph nodes on the occipital bone behind the ears. The blisters are terribly itchy for seventy-two hours and generally spread all over the body. The full breakout takes three days. The first day the blisters are clear; the second day they turn yellow; and the third day they become scabby and brown. They remain for sixteen days.

The incubation period is sixteen days after exposure. A child is not contagious until he breaks out. He should then be isolated from other children. If you know your child has been exposed, isolate him on the fifteenth day after exposure and keep him isolated until you're sure he's not coming down with the illness. No one knows how long an individual with chicken pox remains contagious.

Fever does not accompany chicken pox unless there are excessive pox that inhibit perspiration or infection in the pox. Aspirin can help with fever or pain (for dosages see pages 101–102). If the child runs a high fever, antibiotics may be in order.

Treatment

1. Keep the child from getting too hot; heat intensifies itching.
2. Keeping the child dry inhibits bacteria growth and helps prevent secondary infection and scarring. Don't allow the blisters to get wet for sixteen days. Never use anything abrasive to the skin such as oatmeal baths or other similar treatment.
3. Don't allow him to scratch; keep him covered and clip his fingernails very short.
4. Dabbing the blisters with Caladryl ointment or Calamine reduces itching. It may be applied repeatedly as needed.
5. Give Chlor-Trimeton or Benadryl syrup every eight hours to relieve itching (dosage indicated on next page).
6. If pox get infected, apply Silvadene Cream twice a day directly to the individual lesion, but don't slather it on.
7. If necessity demands wiping pox on any part of the body, be sure to use sterile cotton moistened in sterile water. With girls, if there are pox in the vulva, wipe off the urine.
8. If the child's throat is affected, paint it with Merthiolate or Mercurochrome once a day to prevent infection (see page 79).
9. Offer the child diversions—videos or crafts.

Chlor-Trimeton or Benadryl Dosage

0–6 months:	1/2 teaspoon syrup or a crushed quarter tablet (see page 103)
6 months–adult:	1 teaspoon syrup or a crushed half tablet (see page 103)

I saw a baby with chicken pox just the other day who had been treated with oatmeal baths. He had gotten impetigo and had blisters as big as silver dollars all over his body from infected pox. Keep them dry and they seldom get infected.

One year we battled six bad cases of chicken pox, five simultaneously. The children were terribly itchy and miserable for three days and nights. We dosed them with Chlor-Trimeton and aspirin round the clock and applied Caladryl nonstop. One of us was holding the baby most of her waking hours to keep her from scratching.

It was hard to keep baby Christina's pox cool and dry in the diaper area. I put her in cloth diapers (pinned loosely with no plastic pants) and changed her as soon as I detected wetness. When she soiled herself I wiped her carefully with sterile water and sterile cotton and dried her with fresh cotton. She was congested and had a tendency to drool onto her chest. I kept a cotton bib on her most of the time, changing it and her T-shirt frequently. After meals I wiped around her mouth carefully with sterile water and sterile cotton, always drying with fresh cotton.

After the pox began to heal, I had to resist a mighty urge to ignore Dr. Denmark's advice and give them all a good scrubbing in the tub. I could hardly wait for them to be clean again!

Steven didn't share my sentiment and rather enjoyed his reprieve from soapsuds. At last I happily ushered him into the bathroom and turned on the water.

"Wait, Mommy!" he cautioned, desperately searching for a pox on his stomach. "I'd better not have a bath yet. I'm sure there is still a pox somewhere!"

Do you know why people are afraid to give aspirin with chicken pox? It's because of that case a number of years ago which was so highly publicized. There was a child who had chicken pox and went on to develop diarrhea and vomiting. (Diarrhea and vomiting are not symptoms of chicken pox, of course. Something else was going on.) Anyway, the intestinal symptoms lasted for about four days, and the child's temperature skyrocketed to 106. On the way to the hospital, the child evidently was given one baby aspirin. By the time they took the child to the hospital, it was so dehydrated that it had Reye's syndrome. The Reye's syndrome was obviously due to prolonged vomiting and diarrhea, but they blamed it on the aspirin. There was something terribly wrong with the child if he had a 106 temperature with chicken pox. It may have been encephalitis or septicemia. However, aspirin is not what caused the Reye's syndrome (see page 54–55).

Strep Throat

If any "healthy" throat is cultured it will show evidence of strep. When the body is run down, tired, hungry, or constipated it can't resist the infection. Every bad throat is strep except in the case of diphtheria. When a child has a fever one of the most common causes is an infected throat. Temperature begins to climb around 6:00 p.m. and goes down around 2:00 a.m. To diagnose check with a flashlight for signs of redness and swelling. If the throat is darker in color than the gums, that probably means infection. To see more clearly, you may have to depress the tongue with a spoon and instruct the child to say "ahhh."

Another method is checking for swollen glands. Hold the back of the neck and head with one hand and instruct the child to lift his chin slightly. With the other hand, feel under the jaw for knots.

Treatment

Paint the throat with Mercurochrome or Merthiolate once a day for three days to kill germs and reduce pain (see page 104).

Procedure

1. Twist a piece of sterile cotton around a Q-Tip and dip it in Mercurochrome squeezing off excess until it's almost dry.
2. Depress the tongue with a spoon; have the child say "ahh," and dab the inflamed area. You may need a helper with a flashlight.

Gargling

Gargling twice a day with Listerine or salt water can help. Saline solution: one teaspoon of salt to one quart of water. Any higher concentration can blister the throat. The child may need antiobiotics if he is running a fever. They may also be in order if the sore throat is particularly painful and persistent, even in the absence of fever. Penicillin works best for throat infections.

Most of our serious diseases are a result of three problems: (1) bad throats, (2) bad teeth, and (3) poor diet. Throat infections can affect other organs if they remain untreated and should be taken seriously.

Tonsils

Tonsils are organs in the back of the throat that are absolutely necessary to the infant during his time of nursing. They come together with the uvula as the baby is sucking. When he takes a mouthful of milk, the tonsils move back, the adenoids keep milk from going into his nose, and he swallows it. After the nursing period, tonsils normally atrophy.

There are large crypts in the tonsils which make them balloon if strep or staph goes down into them. Abscesses that medicine can't reach form in the bottom of the crypt. When the medication series is completed, germs migrate back to the tissue, and the child becomes ill again. The problem is similar to that of an abscessed tooth. It's impossible to get medicine into it.

After scarlet fever the tonsils may become infected with hemolytic strep that causes an enormous amount of pus, evident when they are pressed. The child will never be totally well until the tonsils are removed.

A tonsillectomy is also necessary if the child has a mouth-breathing problem or has had scarlet fever and later begins running a fever regularly in the afternoon, indicating rheumatic fever. (Normally adenoids should be removed with the tonsils.)

A little patient had her tonsils removed. The physician inadvertently left behind a tiny piece of tonsil that had a tiny white abscess on it. She developed a big knot in her neck and began to have swelling. We found albumin in her urine, indicating nephritis.

"If you remove the remaining piece of tonsil, the child will recover," I told her doctor. He didn't think it was large enough to be significant. The child became so ill that as a last resort, he finally did

*it. She began to recover and was completely well within a month.
A tooth infection is like that tonsil. It's not much bigger than a
pinhead, but it sure can wreak havoc in the body.*

*In the past, children with Down's syndrome drooled until we learned
to remove their adenoids. When the adenoids were gone, they could
breath through their noses and they stopped drooling.*

Scarlet Fever

Scarlet fever is a hemolytic strep infection. Its symptoms are
usually a bad throat, high fever, and a rash. If you rub your hand
over the child's body, the rash feels like chill bumps. The skin on
the abdomen may appear pink but not show a definite rash. The
tip of the tongue and the roof of the mouth may be red. Penicillin
is generally prescribed.

Occasionally a child may have scarlet fever without a high
temperature. If he exhibits other symptoms of the disease, see a
physician immediately. Scarlet fever is a serious illness.

Infected Ears

If a child complains of earache, particularly after swimming,
press the V-shaped protrusion on the outer part of the ear (above
the earlobe next to his cheek). If pressure increases the pain, he's
likely to have swimmer's ear, a fungus infection that requires a prescription from a physician. In contrast, pain from an abscessed ear
will not typically increase with such pressure. It can actually give
some temporary relief.

Dr. Denmark recommends aspirin and Auralgan for pain. To
administer Auralgan, turn the child on his side and release several

drops, squish them into the ear by pressing gently with your fingers. The effect lasts about four hours. Auralgan does not combat infection but is merely analgesic.

Use ear drops only when there is pain. Sudden relief of pain or blood may indicate a ruptured eardrum, which normally heals within three days without causing deafness. Should the eardrum rupture, put nothing in the ear.

Note: Do not confuse *Auralgan* with *Argyrol*. Auralgan is highly dangerous to the nose or eyes.

If the child runs a fever with an earache and/or the earache is especially severe, he may need ampicillin or penicillin.

Frequently a younger child will cry with an earache until he sits in your lap and presses his ear against your chest. The pressure relieves the pain and quiets the child. If he's put back in the crib, he may begin crying as the pain again intensifies.

Tubes

Allowing tubes to be inserted into a child's ear can actually introduce infection and will permanently damage the eardrum. Tubes are not curative; they merely relieve some of the pressure caused by abscesses resulting from stopped-up Eustachian tubes.

It is far wiser to cure the abscesses with antibiotics and determine what caused the Eustachian tubes to stop up in the first place—commonly colds, allergies, and adenoids. Consumption of milk products and placing babies on carpets often contribute to congestion and ear infections (see Allergies, Chapter Eight).

If a child is old enough to follow instructions to "sniff" in very hard, it sometimes alleviates the earache by clearing the eustachian tubes. Dr. Denmark's system of administering antibiotics every three hours around the clock is a wonderful weapon against chronic ear infections.

If you were a drummer and someone bored a hole in the top of your most expensive drum, could you ever make it perfect again? I doubt it. You would have to purchase a new top for it.

Puncture an eardrum and there will always be scar. Some patients come to my office with pus running out of their ears and down their necks. They were unaware of having infected ears because there was no pressure from the abscess against the eardrums. The pus had made its way around the tubes.

Plastic surgeons try to rebuild eardrums that have been destroyed. Tubes are a money-making thing, but they have never helped any child under the sun.

German Measles

The symptoms of German measles are headache, high fever, and swollen lymph nodes on the occipital bone behind the ears, as with chicken pox. Fever may run continuously for five days. On the fifth day a rash breaks out, usually starting behind the ears and moving to the chest. It then spreads over the entire body. The fever characteristically stops at that time. The rash may not disappear for three to four days, but once it appears the child is no longer contagious. Until the rash breaks out, you can't be certain what the child has, so antibiotics are prescribed early on. Ampicillin is most often used when symptoms are not conclusive. Don't treat the rash, and it's all right to bathe the child.

Pneumonia

As a rule children don't get pneumonia unless they have taken cough syrup or have accidentally aspirated something into their lungs, causing infection to develop. Symptoms are fever, coughing, and rales in the chest that are detectable through a stethoscope. But often you can hear them by pressing your ear on the child's back under the shoulder blades and instructing him to breathe deeply. If he has pneumonia you'll usually hear a "sticky" sound as he inhales. The sound is similar to that of a lock of hair being rubbed between the fingers. Pneumonia is serious. If you suspect your child has it, consult a physician. Penicillin should be administered. Never give cough syrup.

There's no such thing as "walking pneumonia." Well, I take that back. If he has pneumonia and walks to the bathroom, you could say he has "walking pneumonia." If someone walks in my office there's "walking pneumonia." You see, it would be the same pneumonia if he were in bed. I guess there could be "automobile pneumonia." It all depends on how you're getting around!

Sinus Infection

Infection develops when allergies or colds cause the walls of the nasal cavities to stick together. The sinus cavities then become stopped up and abscesses form. Some children's temperatures may climb as high as 106°. If a screaming child has yellow mucus draining from his nose, he likely has a sinus infection. The sinuses, however, may become so stopped up that there is no drainage at all. Clean the nose with Argyrol or saline solution to reduce swelling (see page 72). If the child develops a fever, get a prescription for penicillin or ampicillin.

To avoid such infections, try to determine the causes of your child's allergies and keep them away from him. Common allergens are pollen, smoke, and dust from carpets.

Urinary Tract Infections

If a girl complains of a burning sensation when urinating, first check for redness in her vaginal area. Make sure she isn't using too much soap when she bathes. She may just need to rinse thoroughly with clear water.

Children should not drink anything other than water. Fruit juice produces alkaline urine that can irritate sensitive vaginal tissue, make children susceptible to urinary tract infections, and sometimes cause bedwetting. Note that constant itching in the vaginal area may eventually lead to masturbation. If the condition continues after taking the above precautions, and/or she is running a fever with the same symptoms, she should see a physician and have a urinalysis done.

Macrodantin (an antibacterial medication) is effective with urinary tract infections (cystitis). Dosage for all ages: one teaspoon at each meal three times a day for seven days without stopping until the last day is complete.

Whooping Cough

Whooping cough is a serious, highly contagious disease of the respiratory system which can be prevented by timely vaccinations (see Immunizations, page 29). Children with whooping cough have severe, often frightening coughing attacks every four hours as their bodies try to expel thick globs of egg white-like mucus. The child will choke, gasp for breath, and may even have convulsions brought on by a lack of oxygen to the brain. There is no fever unless a secondary infection develops.

Erythromycin must be given for seven days (for dosages see pages 91–92). It may be necessary to cause the child to gag and cough up mucus before medicine dosages so he will not cough the medicine up. Stimulate the cough by swabbing his throat with a wet cotton swab.

Never use cough syrup. It can actually cause pneumonia (see Coughing, page 73). Even if a child has recovered from whooping cough, he may continue to get bad coughs every time he has a cold for up to one year (see Chapter Thirteen and pages 190–193).

How to Stop Passing the "Bugs" Around

Occasionally one of our children will bring home a highly contagious "bug" and it's passed through the family. Battling such an illness might mean a few sleepless nights for a mother of two. For me it could mean several weeks of sleep deprivation. That's extra incentive to avoid picking up and passing the bugs around!

Healthy children are less likely to catch something. Develop good health habits (see Chapter Eleven). Instruct your children in the practice of good hygiene. Washing hands frequently, covering mouth's when coughing and not sharing cups are some of the obvious rules.

Avoid chills. Be weather-sensitive when you dress your children. Cotton undershirts in winter are good for girls as well as boys.

Separate sick children from healthy ones as much as possible (this is difficult). Certainly do not let them sleep close together.

Keep your kitchen surfaces and bathrooms disinfected and floors clean. When we moved to our present home we replaced carpets with wood parquet and linoleum. Since then we have had significantly less respiratory illness. It is much easier to keep wood and linoleum dust free and clean. I wash my nastiest laundry (diapers, wipe cloths, etc.) with a germicide such as Shaklee Basic-G.

If the baby is sick we sometimes wash and disinfect his toys, too.

You cannot keep your children in a "bubble", but you can avoid taking little ones into public when there is a lot of illness around. Try not to use nurseries. Don't take sick children to church and sweetly encourage your friends not to either.

One fall our whole family attended a great conference. Unfortunately an intestinal bug came home with us which passed through the family not once, but several times. I was desperate. Dr. Denmark instructed me to wipe all the handles and door knobs in the house with alcohol. We placed a hand sanitizer (62% alcohol) on the back of each commode. Everyone was told to use it after a bowel movement even before touching the toilet handle. I used the sanitizer immediately after cleaning vomit or changing diapers. We finally stopped passing the bug around.

Antibiotics 7

"**S**teve, both Leila and Joseph have bad throats, and Dr. Denmark has put them on penicillin. Will you help me tonight? If you dose them at twelve o'clock, I'll do it at three. Don't forget to reset the alarm clock for me. You know what she says about missing a dose."

I've talked to scores of moms who are skeptical of antibiotics. They have related story after story of children taking them for weeks, even months. Often their pediatricians have tried several different kinds, progressing from cheap to very expensive varieties. Still their children do not respond. I hear of maintenance dosages, tubes in the ears, yeast infections.

It's a mystery to me why pediatricians have departed from the original system of administering the antibiotics that Dr. Denmark uses. Instead of the typical four doses per day for ten days, we follow Dr. Denmark's preferred regimen. As a result, our use of antibiotics is short-lived and highly effective. In over twenty years our ten children have never needed tubes in the ears and have almost never had relapses. I seldom have had to repeat a round of antibiotics. This mom is convinced that the original way is the best.

Effective Use of Antibiotics

Antibiotics don't kill germs; they keep them from multiplying. To be most effective, the medication has to be kept in the bloodstream by dosages given **at regular intervals around the clock**. Missing one by fifteen minutes can greatly decrease the medication's effectiveness. If they are always given on time you can expect to see a difference in your child's condition in thirty-six to forty-eight hours. If the child is recovering from flu, it may take a little longer. The regimen must continue for at least seventy-two hours, but it is seldom necessary beyond that. Occasionally a repeat of the whole treatment cycle is indicated.

The following are lists of the medications and dosages Dr. Denmark uses most frequently:

Penicillin

Penicillin is most effective against throat and sinus infections, pneumonia, bladder, kidney, and breast infections, scarlet fever, and sometimes impetigo.

Dosages*

0–4 months:	125 mg (1/2 teaspoon)
4 months–1 year:	125 mg (1 teaspoon)
1 year–adult:	250 mg (1 teaspoon or one tablet)
Adult:	two 250 mg tablets for the first eight dosages (every three hours) and switch to one 250 mg tablet for the remaining 48 hours

* Every 3 hours for 72 hours (around the clock).

Note: If the child is allergic to penicillin, ampicillin may be substituted.

Ampicillin

Ampicillin is most effective in the treatment of ear infections, flu, and meningitis and can also be used as an alternative to penicillin. Children usually prefer the taste of ampicillin, so it is easier to administer. In case of a fever without other conclusive symptoms (not clear what kind of infection is present), it's best to use ampicillin. The dosages for ampicillin are identical to those of penicillin.

Erythromycin

Most effective in the treatment of digestive problems like diarrhea and salmonella poisoning and can be used for whooping cough.

Dosages*
0–4 months:	200 mg (1/8 tsp)
4 months–1 year:	200 mg (1/4 tsp)
1 year–20 years:	200 mg (1/4 tsp)

* Every 3 hours for 72 hours (around the clock).

Note: With whooping cough, dosages continue for seven days.

If the child vomits the medication within twenty minutes, repeat the dose. If there is no more vomiting, continue schedule. Should it continue, stop the medication and try to determine the cause for the vomiting. The child may need an enema, highly effective in such cases. He may be allergic to the medication. In any case the vomiting must be stopped before an antibiotic can be effective. Erythromycin can give children a stomachache. If it's severe, cut the dosage in half.

Allergy to Antibiotics

An allergic reaction to medication is indicated by immediate and repeated vomiting, diarrhea, or rash. A rise in temperature is not symptomatic of an allergy. If you suspect an allergic reaction, discontinue it immediately and contact a physician.

Administering the Antibiotics

Doing it Dr. Denmark's way is admittedly more difficult than the four-daily-doses routine. It is critical that the medication be given precisely on schedule, so it takes discipline on the part of the parents—remembering to set the alarm, getting up in the middle of the night, dealing firmly with a sleepy, resistant child. Inconvenience, however, is a small price to pay for the benefits received.

Tips for Giving Medicine to Young Children

Ask your pharmacist for the best-tasting brand of a particular medicine. I use an oversized dropper that has a rubber ball on the end and is specifically designed for infants. They are available in most drug stores. Our brand is EZY-DOSE. They minimize spilling and enable you to coax the medicine down the child more slowly. For older children I recommend a medicine spoon made in the shape of a tube ending in a "duck bill." They are also made by EZY–DOSE. If your infant (0–4 months) is taking Erythromycin, you may need to purchase a 1/8 tsp. measuring spoon.

Since liquid antibiotics must be kept in the refrigerator, it's colder than a young child is used to. Fill the tube with a dose, put one finger on the end to keep the medicine from spilling, and run hot water over it. That takes the chill off and makes it more palatable.

Some children resist no matter how much they're coaxed or how good-tasting the medicine is. Keep in mind that they are simply too young to understand its importance. There are times a parent must be absolutely firm.

When we first began using antibiotics, patients went to the hospital every three hours for an injection. The results were miraculous. Later we discovered that taking oral doses every three hours was as effective. As time went on physicians decided adhering to a strict three-hour schedule was too much trouble. Besides, parents didn't like waking up at night and, well, it messed up a doctor's practice. It's not financially advantageous if patients recover quickly! But there is simply no way for an antibiotic to be effective unless it is kept in the bloodstream.

Allergies

"**D**r. Denmark,...it's our twelve-year-old...she's broken out all over with a rash like small welts except on her face. New clothes? Well, she did wear a new outfit yesterday, and no, it's never been washed. You're saying she may be allergic to the dye? She does have very sensitive skin."

Identification

The day a person is conceived, lifetime allergies are established. One doesn't develop allergies or grow out of them. They can't be cured, but allergens can be avoided.

Allergy may manifest itself in a variety of ways, including respiratory problems, hay fever, vomiting, diarrhea, migraine headaches, eczema, rashes, clear runny noses, stomachaches, and asthma. It can produce different symptoms at different times. One day a child may have a headache and at another time break out in a rash in reaction to the same allergen. (Fever is evidence of infection, not an allergy.)

Treatment

The first step is to discover the cause (or causes) and keep the child away from it. Use a process of elimination and closely observe him.

Common sources are mold, pollen, smoke, dust, milk products, citrus fruits, and chocolate. Carpets and rugs contain many allergens, so wood floors are much preferable to wall-to-wall carpeting. If your family has a problem with allergies, you might consider replacing carpets with linoleum, tile, or hardwood. Never put an infant down on a carpet even with a blanket beneath him. It can cause congestion and lead to ear infections. Don't use a humidifier because it produces mold. Keep the house as dry and dust free as possible. Use a dehumidifier if necessary. Prohibit smoking indoors.

Avoid the use of lotions, powders, creams, and perfumes and rinse soap thoroughly from skin and clothes. Use a pure soap such as Ivory, or try a variety until you find one that works well for your child's skin. We also use Safeguard with good results. Rinse soap thoroughly. For a child with sensitive skin, wash new clothes before he wears them.

Mothers long ago didn't know the word allergy, but they might say, "Every time he goes to the hen house he gets the wheezies." Another might observe, "Every time he goes to Grandma's and sleeps in the feather bed, he gets the wheezies." Observation is a key ingredient to determining allergies.

Most congestion is a result of an allergic reaction to tobacco smoke, pollen, and mold. During rainy weather a lot of children get stopped up noses. If parents use a vaporizer, the moisture level in the house is increased, producing more mold. The only place steam should be used is in the bathroom with the door closed.

In years gone by we sent children to the desert or to the seashore to cure respiratory problems. The ocean air was fresh, and beach-houses had open windows, spotless linoleum floors, and little dust or mold. It was easier for allergy-prone people to breathe in those environments. When reading the Old Testament we find that the Israelites burned down houses that had mold growing in them. They knew it would make them sick.

Allergies and Infants

Careful observation of a baby on breast milk can identify allergies early on. If he exhibits allergic symptoms, experiment with eliminating various foods from your diet.

Introducing baby foods too early doesn't cause allergies, but don't do so before twelve weeks in any case. An infant isn't able to digest foods properly before then. At twelve weeks the child typically begins to drool, indicating his saliva now contains ptyalin, an enzyme that enables the liver to change starch into sugar. Now begin giving him one new food at a time with careful attention to possible allergic reactions. If a child is allergic to a particular food, he is allergic to very small amounts of it, not just large amounts (see page 18).

An allergy is like stealing. If you take a penny, you might as well have taken a million dollars—it's still sin. A mother says, "Oh, I didn't give him enough to hurt him." She gave him a drop and his body reacted. You can't play around with an allergy. If it's wrong, it's wrong.

Desensitizing Shots

Test series may be helpful in determining allergies, but shots are not effective. If a child receives a skin test series, the mother can try exposing him to some of the substances his skin has shown a sensitivity to. Some of the substances may cause a visible allergic reaction; others pose no problem at all. But the best solution is to discover the allergen and stay away from it.

My husband had severe allergies, so we routinely avoided taking any room on the first floor of a hotel. We knew from experience that the rugs there would be musty. The higher the room, the less mold and dust. We also discovered he was allergic to raw apples. Every time we visited one of his sisters, he came home terribly ill. Though he could eat cooked apples, we finally determined the culprit was the raw ones in her wonderful Waldorf salad.

Antihistamines and Decongestants

Chlor-Trimeton syrup is a good antihistamine (for dosages see pages 102–103). Do not, however, use a decongestant. The body tries to expel foreign matter in the same way eyes tear to expel sand or dust. A decongestant hinders that process.

Emergency

Some allergic reactions are life threatening. If your child begins to have respiratory problems or has welts cov-

ering his body after a bee or wasp sting, take him immediately to the emergency room. With any severe allergic reaction, don't hesitate to consult a physician.

Dr. Denmark's Medicine Cabinet

"**M**ommy, I hate to wake you up, but I can't sleep. My ear is killing me. Can you give me something to make it feel better?"

"Don't worry about waking me, Jessica. Earaches can be pretty painful. Some Auralgen and aspirin should help. I'm sure we have some. If it's not well by morning, we'll have Dr. Denmark take a look at it."

Illnesses and injuries are unpredictable, so every mother needs a locked medicine cabinet stocked with some basic supplies. The following is a list Dr. Denmark recommends keeping on hand. Some dosages are also given. For use of the medicinal items, refer to preceding chapters.

Nonprescriptive Items

Aspirin

for colds, fever (see Chapter Five), headache, earache, menstrual pain, pain due to minor injury, or fever from vaccination

Dosage

1–3 months: dissolve 1 crushed baby aspirin in 5 teaspoons of water; give 1 teaspoon.*

3–5 months: dissolve 1 crushed baby aspirin in 4 teaspoons of water; give 1 teaspoon.*

5–7 months: dissolve 1 crushed baby aspirin in 3 teaspoons of water; give 1 teaspoon.*

7–12 months: dissolve 1 crushed baby aspirin in 2 teaspoons of water; give 1 teaspoon.*

12 months: 1 baby aspirin.* If your 12 month-old will not swallow a tablet, crush it and mix it with water or honey.

12 months–adult: consult bottle for dosage.

* Aspirin should be administered every four hours as needed. It is a safe medication that has been used effectively for over a hundred years. Dr. Denmark is certain that aspirin does not cause Reye's syndrome (for further discussion see pages 54–55, 78).

Caladryl ointment or witch hazel

for itching due to insect bites (see pages 44–46) or chicken pox (see pages 75–78)

Dosage

Apply as needed to reduce itching.

Chlor-Trimeton or Benadryl syrup

for bee stings (see page 44), poison ivy (see page 41), discomfort from chicken pox (see pages 75–78), or minor coughs (see pages 73–74)

Chlor-Trimeton syrup is not commonly stocked. Some pharmacists will order it for you. If your child cannot tolerate Benadryl and you cannot obtain Chlor-Trimeton syrup, try crushing a tablet and mixing it with water, honey or food. One teaspoon of Chlor-Trimeton syrup is equal to 1/2 of a 4 mg Chlor Trimeton tablet (active ingedient: chlorpheniramine maleate).

Dosage*

0–6 months: 1/2 teaspoon syrup or 1/4 of a 4 mg tablet crushed

6 months–adult: 1 teaspoon syrup or 1/2 of a 4 mg tablet crushed

* Normally administered every 8 hours as needed.

Enema bag

for administering enemas (see Chapter Four & kit instructions)

Purchase a douche-enema bag kit, also called a fountain syringe. These may double as a hot water bottle. Not all pharmacies carry them but can order one for you. Use only the enema pipe. Clean enema pipe and inside pipe adapter after each use to remove Vaseline. Residual Vaseline can keep the pipe from screwing into the adapter securely.

If you cannot readily obtain an enema bag kit and are in a hurry, purchase an adult-sized pre-mixed (saline laxative) Fleet enema. The nozzle is small enough for a baby. Dispose of the solution, and rinse the bottle, and use it in place of an enema bag. Since the bottle is small, you will have to refill it and administer the enema more than once. After the bottle begins to collapse, it can help to withdraw the nozzle and unscrew the top so that the bottle fills with air and resumes its shape. Screw the top back, reinsert the nozzle, and squeeze out remaining liquid. Avoid squeezing air into the rectum.

Note: Dr. Denmark does not recommend the prepared, saline laxative Fleet enema for digestive disorders except for severe constipation.

Gauze, Band-Aids, adhesive tape

Listerine

for alleviating sore throats (gargle twice daily)

Cotton swabs

for treating throats (see page 79) and cleaning out noses (see page 72)

Six-inch cotton applicator sticks are much handier to use than the more common Q-Tips but are difficult to find. Ask your druggist for them or call a pharmacy that specializes in hospital supplies.

Mercurochrome or Merthiolate

antiseptic for cleansing wounds and swabbing throats (see page 79)

Unfortunately both of these medications are no longer being marketed. We hope they will become available again.

Milk of Magnesia

for minor stomachaches (see pages 35–36), mild diarrhea or constipation (see page 54)

Also used to prepare the digestive tract for an enema (see pages 54–56).

Pedialyte

for restoring electrolyte balance and preventing dehydration
It can be used effectively at any age (see page 58).

Rubbing Alcohol

for cleansing wounds and disinfecting door knobs, handles, and commode seats

It is good to use when there's a lot of illness in the house (see page 87) or when traveling.

Special medicine spoons (see page 92)

Sterile cotton

for wiping diaper area in newborns, cleansing wounds, cleaning out noses, opening tear ducts, and swabbing throats

Syrup of Ipecac

for inducing vomiting in case of accidental poisoning

Post the telephone number for the local poison control center somewhere near the phone and consult them before administering.

Thermometer

for taking body temperature

Purchase two glass thermometers in case one gets broken (see pages 63–64). After use, wipe the thermometer with alcohol then wash with soap and warm (not hot) water.

Vaseline

for applying to nozzle of enema tube and helping chapped skin (see page 44)

Prescriptive Items

Argyrol

for eye infections (see page 48) and cleaning out noses (see page 72)

Argyrol is presently unavailable on the market. We are hoping it will become available again soon. Research is being done on a substitute for Argyrol. Dr. Denmark has not studied this product and so cannot recommend it. Information on this product can be obtained by contacting Vitamin Research Products at 1–800–877–2447 or www.vrp.com The product is Silvicidal.

Auralgan (Antipyrine, Benzocaine, and Anhydrous Glycerin)

analgesic for earache

Auralgan should never be confused with Argyrol (see pages 81–82)

Mycostatin Powder

for diaper rash (three times a day—see pages 16–17), eczema with a fungal infection (see pages 39–40), athlete's foot (see pages 41–42), or ringworm (see page 42)

Silvadene Creme

for burns, cuts, eczema, impetigo, boils (see pages 37–43)

Available Kitchen Items

Baking soda—for enemas

Salt—for sore throats, tea enemas, cleaning out noses

Karo Syrup—for tea enema

Tea—for tea enema

Bleach—for bee stings, ant bites, poison ivy, jellyfish stings

---

I've used these medicines since they were made and those that work I continue to use. New medications are constantly being developed, and they're wonderful. But as long as my methods and medications are effective, why change?

Mother's Presence

"Do you work, Mrs. Bowman?" When I'm asked that question, I'm tempted to be flippant.

"Work? Why yes as a matter of fact. I was up till four this morning with a sick baby and grabbed two hours sleep before my workday started again. No, I don't usually watch soap operas and eat bonbons. Challenging? Oh, yes. I must stretch my capabilities to the limit. In my job, there are many hats to wear. I am counselor, doctor, teacher, nutritionist, housekeeper, drill sergeant, secretary, and watchdog all rolled into one.

Committed to staying at home? Yes, because I'm convinced my children need me. Despite all my faults and inconsistencies, I provide something no one else can, something they desperately need—a mother's presence.

A mother cat would never leave her kittens to someone else's care. Bird mothers don't push their babies out of the nest until they are old enough to fly, yet an increasing number of American mothers regularly drop their children off at day care.

Daniel Wattenberg, a writer for *Insight* magazine, summarizes results of recent research on infant care. "Evidence is mounting that as the two-earner family has become the norm, parents may have compromised the early development of children. Infant daycare is being linked to emotional and behavioral problems in children."[1] Jay Belsky, professor of human development at Penn State University and former proponent of infant day care writes: "Children who initiated care in the first year...seemed at risk not only for insecurity but for heightened aggression, non compliance, and possibly social withdrawal in the preschool and early school years."[2]

According to Karl Zinsmuster, an adjunct scholar at the American Enterprise Institute: "the loving care of a biological parent, the mother nine times out of ten, is still the best care; accept no substitutions. The child, at least for that first couple of years, has to see a parent most of his waking hours.... Apparently infants cannot cope with regular extended separations in those first couple of years.... There's just no evidence that you can raise children as a hobby on the side and have them come out right."[3]

Dr. Brenda Hunter, psychologist and specialist in infant attachment applauds stay-at-home moms. "These mothers are at home because they know that they, and not a child-care provider, can best nurture their children and give them a sense of home. They know children thrive in their mother's presence and suffer from her prolonged, daily absences.... Babies need their mothers. They need them during their earliest years more than they need babysitters, toys, or the material comforts a second income will buy."[4]

Infants are not the only ones at risk for lack of mothering. In *Can Motherhood Survive?*, Connie Marshner observes:

"Children in America are starving—for love, for attention, for their parents to notice them. Not in a casual way, by giving them more toys. These children learn early that talk is cheap. 'I love you, dear,' from your mom doesn't mean much if you have to hang out at a neighbor's house to find someone who has time to listen to what's worrying you."[5]

Christine Dubois left an exciting job in a corporate office to care for her baby. "After two years away from the office, I still feel the lure of the fax machines and business suits," she reflected. "But I can honestly say I'd rather talk to Lucus than meet with VIP's, rather read 'Humpty Dumpty' than study top-secret memos, rather eat peanut butter and jelly than dine well during power lunches.

"My son is a different person than he was two years ago. And so am I. I've witnessed the everyday miracle of human development, been part of the wonder of discovering Lucus. I've fed and dressed, worried and laughed, comforted and cared. But most important of all, I was there."[6]

Moms, are you listening? Are you there to nourish with your presence and to enjoy the privilege of guiding and watching your children grow? If not, you may be missing the greatest moments of your life. Don't be duped by modern cultural pressures. Don't sell your birthright for a mess of pottage. Make no mistake: children can be frustrating and require a lot of work, but no occupation is without its moments of tedium. There is no greater privilege or joy, no more important occupation than being a mother at home.

Dr. Denmark believes it's absolutely critical to a child's health and well-being that mothers invest their time and energies at home, particularly when children are young. She perceives motherhood to be the most important vocation on earth. She, too, is highly disturbed over the increasing numbers of children who spend most of their waking hours in day care. Her counsel is encouraging, inspiring—and convicting. (What follows is Dr. Denmark's counsel in her own words.)

Responsibility

"Today women are brainwashed into believing there's something greater than being a mother. I surely wouldn't want all women to be mothers, it's too important a job for just anyone. A special person should be a mother. Those who don't want to be mothers, ought to be business women or have some other occupation, but they have no right to bring little babies into the world unless they're willing to stay home and take care of them.

"I'm not the type to be tied down with a baby and a home. I wouldn't be able to take it," a woman once told me. Well, why did she have one in the first place? I would never kill a baby under any circumstances (abortion). If I were to put the baby on the counter and hand the mother a knife and say, "Take its head off..." no woman would do it—not a one. She wants a law passed so somebody else can kill that baby for her, and then she's not to blame. We're looking for excuses in life all the time. If people don't want children, there are lots of ways to keep from having them—like remaining single and living a chaste life.

"A woman can do anything. I'm not against her climbing to the very top. She could be president of the United States as far as I'm concerned. But if she brings a baby into the world, she should take responsibility for it."

Education

"Someone brought me a book entitled, *Why Would a Woman As Smart As You Be at Home?* The theory is that if you have a wonderful education, you should go do something worthwhile with it and let lesser people rear your children. It won't work; it has never worked. A cow never neglects her calf. It would be enlightening for people to study how animals take care of their young until they are grown enough to take care of themselves.

"There's never been a woman too educated to take care of her baby. My mother cared for me, and I didn't have a bit better sense than to take care of my daughter. Mary had an excellent education and could have been a successful businesswoman, but she too stayed home and reared a couple of fine sons.

"America today is a wrecked nation. Eighty-five percent of our children go to day care and learn to fight their way through life. There a child tries to build something and the other children snatch at it and tear it down. He in turn begins snatching and fighting. There is no peace for him. He's not able to have a quiet time at home. He'll not learn to do things by himself or learn self-discipline. He can't develop confidence in anyone because his mother has deserted him. Rejected youngsters will one day ruin our country.

"We must find women willing to stay at home and teach their little children how to read and write, how to stay in their rooms and build something. Children in day care learn to be robots; at home they can learn to be individuals."

Economics

"We've taken the baby out of the cradle and put the economy in it, setting him aside to make money. We're going to make careers and all kinds of things, but we're not making people. Somebody has to be willing to stay home and do that.

"You hear about so many women entering the work force. They think they've found freedom but don't seem to realize they aren't free at all. Working eight hours a day or getting fired makes them more like slaves. If they've earned a million dollars by the time they're sixty-five and never know the joy of rearing children, they haven't accomplished anything.

"I spoke with a woman not long ago whose baby had been in day care ever since he was six weeks old. It cost her four hundred dollars a month and another fifty dollars every week or ten days in doctor bills. The baby was constantly sick. She said she had no choice because she and her husband were buying a house. I asked her how long it would take. They had a thirty-year loan.

"That poor woman comes home every night tired out, to a tired husband and a sick baby. After thirty years, what will she have? She'll probably lose her husband, her house will be out of date, and she'll never have developed a good relationship with her child. She'll never have any of the wonderful pleasures of living. It's better to live in a lean-to and have some of the fun. We've somehow convinced working women they're having a good time. There's no good time to it at all."

The Best?

"Many modern women are determined to provide everything for their children they didn't have when they were growing up. So they find outside employment.

"Is it best for children to have things or to be prepared to use things? Parents might be determined their kids are going to have good houses, cars, education. The best would be for them to teach those children a way of life; then they needn't worry about the rest. I've seen women in the slums who made their sheets out of rags, yet their children went to college.

"I made my way through college without asking my parents for help. What they gave me was a good start. If you give a child a brain you don't have to give him money; he can make it himself. It takes parental care and guidance for a child to develop to his full potential. If he hasn't the necessary mental and emotional maturity, all the money in the world won't enable him to make it in life.

"I don't believe anyone can be too poor to take care of her baby. One of my mothers bore a son out of wedlock. The father wanted nothing to do with her, so she was on her own. She cleaned houses to earn a living and took the baby with her in a basket while she worked. That woman kept her son with her until he was old enough to go to school. He turned out to be a fine young man.

"When I was a child, there were tenant farmers who worked for my father. The women worked with them in the fields, and they also took their babies along in baskets. No leaving them with strangers. My sister was a seamstress. She reared three fine children and never left them. She did her sewing at home."

Attitude

"A woman who would rather be doing something else can't be a good mother. Subconsciously, she'll hate her children because they prevent her from being a lawyer or a doctor or having a big time. I knew a great tennis player who put her baby in day care. If she felt tied down at home when she wanted to be on the court, do you think she would be good to her child? "You children are depriving me of my game today." That's the attitude many children are living under.

"The mental health of mother and child largely depends on her attitude toward her vocation. Today women have been brainwashed into thinking they've been abused since the beginning of time. They resent the fact that they've had to wash diapers, cook, and tend their babies. Nobody mentions how they got the money to buy the diapers and food. They forget about the poor man who plowed all day, wearing himself out in the cold and heat for the income to purchase essentials. We're telling women how abused they were in the past. It's simply not true. Theirs were the happiest homes in the world. Mama was doing what she loved to do, and her husband was making it possible for her to have what she needed."

Relationships

"The most important people in life are our little people, our husbands, and those who looked after us when we were young. Tragically, these are the three classes of people we have discarded. The old people are shut away in nursing homes. Men? We don't need them any more. We can handle our own business, and we're tired of them imposing on us, insulting us. Babies? When they turn six weeks old, we place them in someone else's care. Children are the sorriest, most neglected creatures we have on earth today.

"I see so many women who simply don't want to focus on their homes. They find something outside that they want to do. They've got to go do something 'worthwhile.' They are quite willing to teach other people's children or do volunteer work for a children's hospital, but they just don't want to be 'tied down' with their own children.

"Did you read what Ann Landers wrote about me? She said Dr. Denmark preaches that a woman should not pursue a career and look after her children, but Dr. Denmark is a professional woman herself. Ann Landers didn't realize that I am preaching what I practiced. Sure, I'm a professional. I had plenty of help with housework, but my office was next to my home, and no else looked after my daughter. I fed her and put her to bed; she played outside my window. I had breakfast with my husband and supervised things at home. I avoided the myriad activities other women doctors got involved in simply because my first obligation was to my family. I made a vow when I married Eustace that I would be a good wife to him. We had a glorious time together.

"I don't believe I would be able to handle my career the same way today and still care for a child. No, it would be impossible to be an attentive mother under present circumstances. Good domestic help is too scarce, and modern-day medical practice is structured differently."

Grandparents

"If a mother can't look after her children for some reason, then a working Grandma should retire and do it for her. Had my daughter been unable to care for her sons, I would have given up medicine. It didn't mean anything to me in comparison to my grandsons. Unfortunately, grandparents no longer feel a responsibility to their grandchildren. They act as though they have paid their dues when it comes to child rearing.

"Grandparents are the Supreme Court for their grandchildren. They should model decent behavior, dress, eat, and speak well. Many aren't very good models. I see grandmothers coming to my office in tight, short skirts with cigarettes hanging out of their mouths. Nobody ever finishes paying his dues. People always have a responsibility toward one another, especially family."

John Eustace Denmark

"Something has burned me up for years. My husband is the one who made it possible for me to practice medicine the way I have. I never had to worry about expenses or providing an income, so I could donate my time to the poor. If it hadn't been for Eustace, I wouldn't have been able to charge my regular patients so little. I've been awarded many honors, but he never received a bit of credit. He was responsible for any accomplishments I have attained. I couldn't have done it without him. Don't you think the Creator should be praised more than the created?"

Home

"All the women who have climbed to the top in society (in medicine, law, and business) and haven't had the experience of rearing their own children...well, when they turn sixty five some-body will throw them a fancy retirement party; then they'll be left with nothing.

"I had a friend years ago who was a wonderful doctor, made a great income, and lived in a beautiful home. She never married. When she retired no one ever cared enough to visit her.

"'If you had your life to live over again, would you live it the same way?' I asked her shortly before she died.

"'No, I wouldn't,' she replied emphatically. 'I've never had any of the things that bring true happiness—a husband or a child. I've never really had a home.'"

Expert Advice and Parenting

"We have been duped into believing that no one knows any-thing but so-called experts—doctors, psychiatrists, news commen-tators. When I was a young doctor, I knew it all. Of course I did because I had just finished medical school. I had all the answers, that is until Mary was born.

"One of these highly educated, really important women called me the other morning. 'Dr. Denmark,' she said, 'I've been thinking about some of the advice you give on feeding children. You know the authorities think you are wrong. They say a baby should nurse on demand and children should eat six times a day.'

"'Just who on earth is the authority? That word is a funny one, isn't it?' I said to her.

Mrs. Cow never asked Mrs. Pig how to take care of her baby. I believe a woman is as smart as a cow. Surely she can care for her baby as well as a cow looks after a calf.

It's a queer thing—a cow never read a book, never watched a TV documentary, never read a parenting magazine or asked a doctor how to parent. I believe if we just use our heads, we can take care of our young instead of wrecking them as we do.

"When I was a young girl there was a doctor who lived behind our property. Dr. Bowen was one of our dearest friends and later helped me through medical school. When one of the family was ill, he'd come over and ask my mother, 'Alice, what's wrong? What do you think we ought to do?' She'd tell him what she thought, and that's the way it went. Alice did the doctoring.

"A beautiful woman came to my office not too long ago with a baby who looked like the wrath of God. She was feeding it all day long and not having any fun. I questioned her about her background. Evidently, her own family had been terribly poor, but her mother had taken the time to prepare three decent meals a day. I looked at the woman and then back at her baby. That woman didn't need me; she needed her mother. If she'd listen to her, she could have a healthy baby just as her mother had. We don't need doctors any more; we need parents.

"Nowadays we have everything under the sun to keep children healthy—money, clean water, baby food, blenders, medicine—everything except parents.

"So many people today are like broken dishes. Individuals like the late Mother Theresa and James Dobson are trying to glue the pieces back together. Some of the plates will look whole and might even become usable. But a repaired plate will never serve as if it had never been damaged in the first place. It will never be strong enough. Wouldn't it be better to keep plates from being broken? If a mother takes the time to give her child a chance, instead of becoming a broken dish the child will always remain whole."

Notes

1. "The Parent Trap," *Insight* (March 2, 1992), 6.
2. Jay Belsky, "Homeward Bound," *Focus on the Family* (January 1992), 7.
3. "The Parent Trap," 9.
4. "Homeward Bound," 6.
5. Connie Marshner, *Can Motherhood Survive?* (Brentwood, TN: Wolgemuth and Hyatt, 1990), 11.
6. "Romancing the Mom," *Focus on the Family* (February 1993).

Nutrition and Health Habits

Reading books and articles on nutrition can be terribly frustrating for a mother. The nutrition experts change their recommendations every few years or even months as new research is completed. Not only is the advice we receive through the media changeable, the prices at grocery stores are downright depressing. Does a family have to be wealthy to be healthy?

Dr. Denmark always emphasizes the importance of good nutrition and a healthy life style, but conversing with her has given me the confidence that my children can be healthy if we stick to simple meals and common sense health habits. The excellent health Dr. Denmark has enjoyed for over one hundred years is convincing testimony to her understanding of what a body truly needs.

Many people take better care of their cars than they do of their own bodies. They would never dream of using the wrong kind of fuel, yet they consistently put the wrong kind of food in their mouths.

Nourishment

Good nutrition is absolutely fundamental to health and happiness. A growing child particularly needs three balanced meals a day.

Protein

Each meal should contain high-quality protein. The best sources are lean meat, eggs, and black-eyed peas. All legumes have protein, but black-eyed peas have the most. Other legumes may be interspersed with meat and black-eyed peas. Lean red meat is healthful because of its high iron content. One egg a day won't harm anyone who is eating a balanced diet. Two eggs for breakfast are fine for children. For those who dislike eggs, it's all right to substitute other proteins. You can also disguise the taste of eggs in French toast (see page 129), or by boiling a beaten egg in oatmeal. Don't be a slave to your child's desires, but exercise some creativity in encouraging him to enjoy healthful foods.

Incidentally, if anyone has difficulty getting moving in the morning, consider whether he is eating enough protein at supper.

During World War I research was done on legumes and other meat substitutes. It was discovered that black-eyed peas had the most protein. We tried peanut butter—it's better than nothing, but it isn't as good as some of the other proteins. If you eat a good protein, you're not hungry till the next meal. However, if you eat a carbohydrate meal with no protein, you build a lot of insulin. On a breakfast of just a roll and orange juice, in two hours you have hypoglycemia. Then a teaspoon of sugar might keep you going beautifully for another two hours. It's killing you, but that's all right—the undertaker needs a job.

If you moved every time a child moved, I think you'd burn up a good bit of cholesterol. I see no harm in an egg, it's nothing but chicken. I've had an egg every morning for one hundred years. One a day won't hurt anybody.

No, I don't think there's anything wrong with eggs, but people do take things to extreme. I had a boy come to my office one day. He was 12 years old and weighed 225 pounds. I checked his blood pressure. It was 200/100. He was senile. I questioned him about his meals, and he said he ate a dozen eggs and a loaf of bread for breakfast. Everything that God made on earth, He made good. However, anything can be taken to extreme. Even water...you can drink enough water to commit suicide.

There's nothing wrong with red meat. It contains an enormous amount of the iron we need in our diet. At one point people wouldn't buy chicken because they didn't want the dark meat, so farmers started raising milk-fed chickens that were so anemic there wasn't enough red blood in the thigh to make it dark. The chickens had more white meat, but the thighs weren't as good as they would have been had they eaten normally.

Starches

Every meal should contain a starch. Whole grains and potatoes are the best sources. Homemade whole grain breads and cereals are a great addition to any family's diet (see pages 136–137).

Whole grains are very important. Nowadays we take the vitamins out of food, put them into a bottle, and sell them.

Vegetables

At both lunch and supper, a child needs a serving of vegetables, especially green and leafy ones that contain iron. Alternate them with yellow vegetables like corn and squash. Though fresh produce may have a higher vitamin content, frozen or canned varieties are perfectly acceptable. Frozen vegetables are convenient and contain few additives or salt. Cooked vegetables are as good as raw ones and are actually easier to digest.

Hematocrits are done on children to show the number of red blood cells they have. It doesn't matter how many cells there are unless the cells contain enough heme to transport sufficient oxygen. Bringing a hundred empty train cars into a starving Atlanta would be purposeless; the cars have to be loaded with good food. It is the same with hematocrits. The amount of heme in the cells needs to be determined. People need the heme obtained from leafy green vegetables, lean meat, and whole grain bread.

Fruit

Fruit is not vital to nutrition. When a family is limited in its food budget, bananas and apples may be the best choices. Citrus tends to be overrated in its nutritional value. In years gone by, fruit was only eaten in season. Dr. Denmark's recommended diet for infants (see pages 18–23) contains a great deal of fruit simply because infants will eat vegetables and proteins more readily if they are mixed with fruit. Infants love food that is akin to breast milk. Like breast milk, it needs to be sweet and warm.

When I was a child we didn't have oranges in this part of the country. We each received an orange in our stocking at Christmas and that was all. So many times when people are grocery shopping they focus on oranges, grapes, and the like, but their money would be better spent for good vegetables, lean meat, and whole grain starches.

We've run this fruit business into the ground. Your great-grandma never had any fruit at all except in season. Fruit is all right, but there are other foods which are more necessary.

Sweets

Honey as a sweetener is far superior to sugar. Even sugar in limited amounts is not harmful to the average child. A sweet dessert once or twice a week won't hurt, but children should not expect to have them every day. Dessert on Friday night or for Sunday dinner makes the meal special and gives children something to look forward to.

Everything's good until man makes it bad. There's nothing wrong with sugar unless it's eaten to excess. As a young person, I was a sugar addict. I began to develop arthritis at thirty-five. My joints became sore, and I had pain in my hips. At fifty I eliminated sugar from my diet, and my hand is still as limber as any sixteen year-old's. I can touch the floor without bending my knees.

Drinks

Don't drink anything but water and drink when you're thirsty. So many are saying we need eight or more glasses of water a day. I don't think that's necessary. There is actually something called water intoxication. The blood can get so diluted that there are not enough electrolytes to make the heart beat (see page 15). *We used to have a bucket on the back porch and people drank when they were thirsty. Individual needs can vary.*

The family should not drink anything but water. Even fruit juices should be eliminated because of their concentrated fructose content. It's preferable to give a child fruit rather than juice. Fiber and protein in the pulp provide a much more balanced food. Juice stresses the kidneys and produces highly alkaline urine that can cause burning, itching, and even urinary-tract infections.. Drinking water exclusively can sometimes cure a bedwetting problem.

I wouldn't give a child anything to drink except water. I had a little boy in my office not long ago. He looked like the wrath of God. I tested his urine. I've never seen that much sugar in any human's urine. "Where in the world is he getting this sugar?" I asked his mother.

"We don't let sugar come into our house," she said. She was one of those health nuts.

"What does he drink?"

"Apple juice. I make it myself."

"What do you do with the pulp?"

"I throw it on the mulch pile."

I calculated that the child was getting eight ounces of pure sugar daily. I'm sure his eyesight was ruined.

"But it's natural sugar!" his mother said.

What sugar isn't natural sugar? The sugar mashed out of canes is natural. Everything on earth is natural! She was taking all the pectin, cellulose, and protein in that apple and throwing it away. The only thing the child was getting was the sugar and water.

People don't understand that children don't need juice. Why not buy the apple instead of just the juice? Why not buy the orange or the carrot and get the whole thing?

Dairy Products

Dairy products are much overrated in the American diet, they should never be a meal's main ingredient. Cheese isn't a good meat substitute, yogurt and cottage cheese not much better. Milk consumption produces anemia. A little cheese sprinkled on top of a casserole, ice cream at a birthday party, or milk in a white sauce occasionally won't be harmful. But anyone past seven months shouldn't drink milk. Guard against regular consumption of dairy products in general. A good margarine is a better choice than butter. If a child is allergic to dairy products, even a small amount cooked with his food is detrimental to his health.

My theory is that too much calcium inhibits absorption of iron. There has been a lot of research done on anemia. We know what causes it in calves—feeding them milk beyond the weaning point to make veal. It's not simply that the animal fills up on milk and neglects other food. We found that if a dog is given a pint of milk along with its regular diet, its hemoglobin drops ten points within a month. Some physicians claim that anemia is caused by bleeding from the colon. I don't agree. I believe it has something to do with absorption.

A three-inch square of cheese is equivalent to a glass of milk. A pizza contains a whole angle of cheese. It's one of the greatest assets to our medical profession. Pizzas produce more coronaries which in turn benefit cardiologists and surgeons. They make kids anemic and benefit pediatricians. Well, it takes the foolish to make the rich rich.

When I was a youngster, we never saw milk on our table. Cows had very small udders and didn't produce much. Later, breeding produced cows with large udders and everyone started drinking lots of milk. We began to develop pellagra.

We first began to buy loaf bread seventy years ago. At that time, "milk toast" became a fad. People would take a big slice of loaf bread, butter it, and toast it. They sprinkled sugar on it and poured milk over it. They might add a little vanilla or lemon to it. Well, people who ate a lot of it began to have diarrhea; they became anemic and started acting rather foolish. Some were actually sent to asylums. They had developed pellagra.

A doctor in Alabama began giving his pellagra patients cabbage pot liquor with wonderful success. We discovered that vitamin B, essential for good nutrition, was the missing ingredient in milk toast.

A mother brought her child in late one afternoon. She had had diarrhea for several weeks. The corners of her mouth were raw and bleeding. Her hemoglobin was 5. She should have died in her sleep. I didn't finish my examination but sent her directly to the hospital for a transfusion. This child had a severe case of pellagra. The mother informed me that she would eat nothing but cheese and white bread.

If I had a child like that, I would not say to her, "You can't have it." Instead I would say, "Sweetheart, we don't have any white bread or cheese in the house." Serve the right foods at meals, at the right time, and don't talk about it. I've never had any trouble feeding children.

Calcium

Calcium intake is much overemphasized. Most foods contain plenty of it.

A lot of widows develop osteoporosis in their old age, but it's not for lack of calcium. Without husbands to cook for, they snack and don't eat a balanced diet. Osteoporosis is caused by a lack of vitamin D necessary for the body's utilization of calcium. Vitamin D is obtained through sunshine, meats, vegetables, and codfish.

Fats

Avoid cooking with fat and cholesterol-laden oils, but a little vegetable oil for flavoring or even some bacon cooked with beans, soups, or greens isn't harmful. The key is moderation. When regular physical labor was a routine part of life, people could tolerate a higher fat content in their diets and remain healthy; it was burned off. Today we are too sedentary to consume much fat.

Mealtime

Meals should be spaced five and a half hours apart, allowing time for the stomach to empty. If a child snacks throughout the day, that never happens. The stomach will not release undigested food other than sugar, so his body is unable to make use of what he eats and he is constantly hungry. He also may be "pot bellied." Even nutritious snacks should not be permitted between meals.

Mealtimes should be happy, with your family sitting down together to thank God for the food and talking about the day. The dinner table is a wonderful place to draw closer, to learn and grow together, to discuss spiritual truths and principles.

It's best not to discuss the food (personal likes and dislikes). You needn't ask the children what they want or don't; you can't be a short-order cook. The plates should be served with sensible portions of everything and placed in front of each child. If there is something all the children particularly dislike, use other foods of similar value; for example, broccoli instead of brussel sprouts, raw carrots instead of cooked.

Don't ever say to your husband, "Forget giving Suzie her beans. She won't eat them. If you say that in front of her, she'll never eat them again. You can put ideas in children's heads. If they never know any better, they eat right. Once they discover refusing food produces chaos, they won't touch it.

I had a patient who wouldn't eat anything but cornbread. Well, his mother bought some baby food. She put pureed string beans and meat into corn muffins for her child. He ate them and had a good time.

A busy mom should focus on simplicity and good nutrition. There's nothing wrong with cooking more than enough for supper and having the rest for lunch the following day.

You needn't provide a gourmet meal every evening. It's fine to eat the same simple dishes often. They are less time consuming, more economical, and usually more healthful. Feasting should be reserved for special occasions.

Your great-grandma awakened and served breakfast at daylight. There was no refrigeration, and no one ate anything else until lunch at midday; likewise, supper. Those old people who were reared on three meals a day have tried dying at nursing homes. They built such good bodies they keep on living. Today we eat all day long, so kids are anemic and don't develop mentally as they should. Mother after mother tells me her family never eats in the morning. I can't imagine children getting up and not having breakfast with Mama and Papa before going off to school. Breakfast is the most important meal of the day.

Sample Menus

Breakfast (should include a protein and a starch)

- boiled egg, oatmeal
- French toast with honey
- fried egg, toast, banana*

It's best not to use milk in preparing French toast. Place a piece of whole wheat bread in a saucer and pour a beaten egg over it. Allow the bread to soak up all the egg. Fry it on both sides in a little margarine.

Lunch (should include a protein and a starch)

- chicken sandwiches, green salad, apple*
- black-eyed peas, brown rice, cabbage
- lentil soup with vegetables, muffins

Supper (should include a protein, starch, and vegetable)

- lean beef, potatoes, broccoli
- baked beans, corn bread, yellow squash
- beef stew, fruit salad*

* Fruits are the least important ingredient for a good daily diet.

In conversation with a young pediatrician at a medical meeting, I remarked that the most important thing a pediatrician should do is teach a mother how to feed and care for her children. I emphasized how much better it was to teach them how to keep their children well rather than simply hand them another prescription.

In response to my words the young man threw up his arms and said, "They don't pay us for that!"

You know it might be better to take a child to a vet. Vets insist on good nutrition for their patients. The vet is very cognizant of the fact that food means everything.

One-dish Meals

We eat a lot of one-dish meals. They are easy to prepare; simple to serve, and contain all the essential foods. Here are a few of our Dr. Denmark-approved favorites.

Beef Stew

Combine:

> 2 lbs. stew beef cut in 1 inch cubes
> 5 carrots sliced
> 1 large onion diced
> 3 stalks celery sliced
> 2-3 potatoes cubed
> 1 28 oz. can tomatoes
> 1 clove garlic crushed
> 2 bay leaves
> salt and pepper to taste

Cook all day in a slow cooker.[1]

Lentil Stew

Combine:

2 cups lentils (rinsed and sorted)
8 cups water
1 onion chopped
3 carrots chopped
1/3 head cabbage chopped
1 tsp. salt
1/4 tsp. pepper

Simmer approximately 20 minutes until lentils are tender.
Add 2 tablespoons oil (we use olive oil).
Simmer 10–15 minutes.

Lebanese String Beans (can use peas or fresh lima beans also)

Sauté two medium onions in olive oil.
Add:

1 28 oz. can tomatoes
2 cans (or fresh equivalent) string beans
4 tsp. chicken bouillon powder
1 or 2 tsp. lemon pepper
1/4 tsp. pepper

Simmer until flavors are blended and vegetables are tender.
Add leftover pieces of beef, chicken, or 1 to 2 lbs. crumbled tofu.
Serve over rice.

Grandma Hart's Famous Noodle Soup

Simmer, covered for 1 1/2 hours:

1 large chicken
14 cups water

    1 tbsp. salt
    1/2 tsp. pepper
    1/2 tsp. basil
    1 bay leaf

Remove chicken and bay leaf; skim fat off broth.
Add to broth:

    6 medium carrots, sliced
    3 stalks of celery, sliced
    2 onions, sliced

Simmer for 45 minutes.

While broth is simmering, cool chicken, debone and cut in bite-size pieces.

Add chicken and 3 cups of uncooked noodles to broth during the last ten minutes of cooking.

Sprinkle with 1/4 cup chopped parsley (optional).[2]

Six-layer Dish

Layer in order in a large greased casserole, seasoning each layer with salt and pepper:

    4 medium potatoes sliced
    2 cups frozen peas or other vegetable
    2/3 cup uncooked rice
    2 medium onions sliced
    2 lbs. browned and drained ground beef
    2 qts. canned tomatoes

Sprinkle with 2 tbsps. brown sugar.

Bake at 300° for 2 1/2 to 3 hours until rice and other vegetables are done.[3]

Chicken and Dumplings

Cover with water and boil for one hour:

> 1 whole chicken (4 to 5 lbs.)
> 1 chopped onion
> 1/8 tsp. cinnamon

Cool and debone chicken.
Skim fat off broth.
(Broth should yield approximately 4 quarts.)
Add to broth:

> 1 package mixed frozen vegetables (or equivalent fresh)
> 3 cubed potatoes
> chicken
> salt and pepper to taste

Simmer for 25 minutes until potatoes are tender.

Make your own dumplings or use canned refrigerator biscuits cut into fourths.

Drop dumpling dough by spoonfuls into vegetable-chicken mixture. Cook 10 minutes uncovered and 10 minutes covered. Add them while vegetables are still cooking to save time.

Dumplings:

> 3 tbsp. shortening or margarine
> 1 1/2 cups flour
> 2 tsp. baking powder
> 3/4 tsp. salt
> 3/4 cup milk

Cut shortening into flour, baking powder, and salt until mixture resembles fine crumbs.

Stir in milk.

Bean Dishes

Prep for beans:

Wash and sort beans, picking out the disfigured ones.
Put beans in a saucepan and cover with about two inches
  of fresh water.
Boil for 2 minutes.
Turn off heat, cover and let sit for one hour or soak overnight.
Drain liquid.

Beans are ready to cook.

Black Beans

Combine in pressure cooker:

1 lb. washed and soaked black beans
6 cups chicken broth
1 onion chopped
3 carrots sliced
1 bay leaf
1 tsp. oregano
2 potatoes chopped
1/2 tsp. garlic powder
1/4 tsp. pepper

Cook with steady hissing for 35 minutes. Let pressure drop
of its own accord.

Just before serving add 3 tbsp. lemon juice.[4]

Bowman Black-eyed Pea Stew

Combine in a pot:

1 lb. washed and soaked black-eyed peas

1/4 head cabbage chopped
1 16 oz. can tomatoes
3 potatoes cubed
3 carrots diced
1 onion sliced
9 to 10 cups water
2 tsp. salt
1/2 tsp. pepper
3 tbsp. olive oil
1 clove garlic crushed

Add sliced yellow squash and zucchini to make it even nicer. Simmer for 20 minutes.

Other Legume Recipes

We eat a lot of legumes for economy and nutrition. I often do them in a pressure cooker or a slow cooker all day. Black-eyed peas and lentils soften more quickly than other legumes. Here are some more of our favorite bean recipes. Add a starch and a vegetable to one of the following dishes to serve a nutritionally complete meal.

Black-eyed Peas

Put in saucepan:

1 lb. soaked black-eyed peas
2 tsp. salt
2 tbsp. oil (we use olive oil)

Can also add onion and garlic for extra flavor.
Barely cover with water.
Simmer for 15 or 20 minutes and serve over rice or with whole grain bread.

Kidney Beans

Combine in pressure cooker:

> 1 lb. washed and soaked kidney beans
> 1 16 oz. can beef broth
> 1 16 oz. can tomatoes
> 1 chopped onion
> 1 tbsp. chili powder
> 1 tsp. salt

Barely cover with water.

Mix ingredients.

Cook in pressure cooker 25 minutes with cooker hissing consistently. Let pressure drop of its own accord.

Baked Beans with Molasses

Combine in pressure cooker:

> 1 lb. washed and soaked beans (Northern, navy, or other)
> 1/4 lb. diced bacon (or 1/3 cup bacon-flavored TVP)
> 3 tbsp. brown sugar
> 3 tbsp. molasses
> 1 tsp. salt
> 1/2 tsp. mustard
> 1 onion chopped
> 2 tbsp. catsup

Barely cover with water.

Cook with steady hissing 45 minutes. Let pressure drop of own accord.[5]

Debra Ridings's Whole Wheat Bread

Grind* 12 cups of whole wheat berries (half Hard Red and half Hard White).

Turn oven to warm and insert dough hook into dough maker.*
Measure 6 cups of flour into dough maker. Add:

2 tbsp. salt
2 tbsp. fresh yeast
1/3 cup gluten
2/3 cup cooking oil
2/3 cup honey
1/3 cup lecithin
1/4 cup ground flaxseed (optional)
6 cups warm water (100°–110°F)

Turn mixer on low speed until all ingredients are pretty well blended. Then increase the mixer's speed and add flour by half cupfuls, mixing well after each addition. When the dough starts to clean the side of the bowl, stop adding flour and set the mixer for 8 minutes.

While the dough is kneading, spray four bread pans with non-stick coating. Lightly oil hands and the surface for shaping the loaves.

When the dough maker is finished kneading remove the dough, divide and shape it into four loaves.

Place the dough in pans and let it rise in the warm oven until doubled in size (our oven takes 33 minutes). Do not open the oven door once the dough is "proofing" or it will collapse. Check on the loaves using the oven light.

Turn the oven temperature to 350° and bake until the loaves sound hollow when tapped on the top (our oven takes 45 minutes).

Butter the tops of the loaves and let them cool in the pans for 10 minutes.

Remove the loaves from the pans.[6]

* We use a Grain Master Whisper Mill and DLX2000 dough maker by Magic Mill.

Everything is made good until man makes it bad. He does what tastes good and feels good even if he kills himself in the process.

Hors d'oeuvres, they really save a meal. A hostess doesn't have to cook as much for her guests because hors d'oeuvres kill their appetite. By the time the guests have a few drinks and hors d'oeuvres, the hostess doesn't have to worry about the main meal. It's a trick! It works two ways—it saves food and it wrecks health, thereby helping doctors make a living.

I've always enjoyed riding horseback in the mountains. We'd see the pretty rhododendron and mountain laurel. The leaves are a beautiful green; so gorgeous. Why won't that horse just take one bite of those leaves? They're poisonous. No, he wouldn't touch them! He'll eat the grass and the briars. But a man, he'll take just a taste. He'll say, "I just have to have a little of those green leaves."

Routine

Children need the security of routine. There should be regularly scheduled meals, naps, work, play, and bed times. Our Creator designed an orderly universe. Spring always follows winter. Day follows night (Gen. 8:22). Even the animals follow their own instinctive routines (Psalm 104:19–30). We humans would be wise to follow suit. Our bodies function best on routine, allowing us to be more productive long term.

A routine understood by all members of the household promotes peace. Most children would not object to naps if they came at the same time every day. All the family would be happier and healthier if parents exercised the discipline of eating at regular intervals and going to bed at a sensible hour. Are we "making straight paths for our feet"?[7] So many headaches, stomachaches, and short tempers could be avoided simply by eating and sleeping according to a consistent schedule.

Routines aren't etched in stone. Life brings many interruptions and sometimes crises. You can't neglect hospitality if friends drop by at mealtimes. Babies don't become ill on schedule. If, however, a family has developed a basic set of good habits, occasional interruptions won't destroy them. When interruptions and crises pass, order is quickly restored.

It's best to establish household schedules in conjunction with your husband's work schedule.

Dr. Denmark recommends the following:

6:00 a.m.	Wake-up time
7:00 a.m.	Breakfast
9:00 a.m.	Baby's naptime
12:30 p.m.	Lunch
6:00 p.m.	Supper, bedtime for baby afterwards

At our house we follow an adapted version that works well.

6:00 a.m.	Mom and Dad wake-up time
6:30 a.m.	Children wake up
7:00 a.m.	Breakfast
	Family worship
	Chores
10:00 a.m.–1:00 p.m.	Home schooling and naptime for babies
1:00 p.m.	Lunch; playtime
4:00 p.m.	Prepare supper
6:00 p.m.	Evening chores (everyone)
6:30 p.m.	Supper
7:00 p.m.	Bath and bed for young children
9:00–10:00 p.m.	Bed for older children

Sleep

It is vain for you to rise up early.
To retire late.
To eat the bread of painful labors;
For He gives to His beloved even in his sleep.[8]

The Creator has told us we need rest. We need to rest on Sunday and maintain good sleeping habits. If our bodies don't get sufficient rest, there are inevitable consequences: fatigue, depression, short temper, increased susceptibility to illness, discouragement, anxiety. The list could continue. When the prophet Elijah was afraid and discouraged, God dealt with his physical exhaustion before he encouraged and instructed him verbally.[9]

Children grow in their sleep and require plenty of undisturbed rest to realize their full growth potential. Without it they will be unable to learn properly during waking hours. As always, maintain a balance. Some people, especially adolescents, have a tendency to sleep too long, though individual sleep requirements vary. Be sensitive to your children's particular needs.

Average Sleep Requirements

Newborn:	20 hours
3 months:	16 hours
2 years:	12 hours
6 years:	12 hours
adolescent:	8 hours
adult:	8 hours

Sunshine and Exercise

Encourage your children to play outdoors. When an infant is two weeks old, take him out in the sun for five to ten minutes daily.

But as we all know, overexposure to the sun's rays is harmful to the skin. Be sensible and don't allow your children to overdo it. Dr. Denmark recommends covering them with hats and clothing rather than using a sunscreen.

When I came to Atlanta in 1928, there were innumerable cases of rickets due to the sheet of smoke that covered the city. The trains puffed and furnaces burned soft coal. People kept house lights on and had mustaches by 10:00 a.m. Kids' arms and legs were bowed. They were obtaining plenty of calcium from evaporated milk but had rickets because their skin lacked exposure to sunshine. People, especially fair-skinned individuals, should never bake in the sun. We do, however, need a certain amount of sunshine for vitamin D.

Encourage exercise by providing a few basic toys like balls, jump ropes, bicycles, or skates. Given the opportunity, most healthy children will get all the exercise they need on their own. Some, however, tend to be sedentary and need more stimulation. Parents can be creative in motivating inactive children, possibly with an outdoor playhouse, exercising a pet, or taking soccer lessons.

Guarding Our Children's Health

In the days before immunizations and antibiotics, infant mortality was 162.4 per thousand births (1900).[10] My great-grandmother lived with constant concern for her infant's health. Letters she wrote to her mother reveal her vigilance in protecting him. She shielded him from chills; was anxious that he receive enough fresh air and sunshine, guarded against germs. She paid particular attention to what he ate and saw that he had plenty of sleep. If her son was ever ill, she was meticulously careful in nursing him back to full recovery. The stakes were too high not to be careful. Serious diseases were commonplace, and so were infant tombstones.

With the advent of modern medicine, infant mortality was 8.9 per thousand births by 1991.[11] What a miracle! But mothers have become complacent and are no longer as conscientious as their predecessors were. That youngsters get adequate rest, nourishment, sunshine, and nursing care isn't a priority in many homes, yet such laxness is detrimental to their long-term health. To reach their full potential physically and mentally, children must build sturdy bodies through good health habits—bodies that last far beyond childhood into ripe old age.

Infants and young children grow at an enormous rate, and sickness interrupts their growth. When they become ill, let's nurse them to full recovery before dragging them out in public. Let them stay home and rest, be quiet, have a chance to heal.

Is your child sick with a fever? Give him a warm bath, fresh pajamas. Change the sheets on his bed. Give him a special book or game to play with, but be sure he rests. He should be fever-free for two evenings before resuming normal activities. It's best for him and for the other children who are exposed to him. When recovering from an intestinal problem, he should have easily digestible food for a few days. A child getting over the flu should stay out of public for one week to allow his immunities to rebuild.

Illness can draw a family together, offer opportunity to show love for your child, and increase his sense of security. Remember, we are building bodies for the future.

I think with gratitude of the excellent nursing care I received from my mother when I was sick. There were hot baths, clean sheets, quietness, good food, and cheerful words. Certainly I despised medicine, needles, and other discomforts and protested them vigorously. Down inside, though, I knew they were in my best interest. There was a wonderful comfort in knowing I was well looked after.

Notes

1. *Rival Cook Pot Cookbook*, 16.
2. Gloria Repp, *Noodle Soup* (Greenville, SC: BJU Press 1994), 28-29
3. Doris Janzen Longacre, *More-With-Less Cookbook* (Scottdale, PA: Herald Press, 1988), 137.
4. Recipe on back of Jack Rabbit Black Turtle Beans.
5. *Presto Pressure Cooker* (Eau Claire, ?: Johnson Printing, Inc., 1979), 51.
6. Debra Ridings, *Feeding the Shepherd's Flocks* (Kearney, NE: Morris Press 1999), 6.
7. Hebrews 12:13
8. Psalm 127:2
9. 1 Kings 19:3–18
10. *Historical Statistics of the United States: Colonial Times to 1970* (Washington, D.C.: Government Printing Office, 1975).
11. *Statistical Abstracts of the United States* (Washington, D.C.: U.S. Department of Commerce, 1994).

The Needs of Children

It was Monday. One glance at the calendar filled me with dread. What a schedule for the week! Doctor's appointments, piano lessons, evening meetings, ballet rehearsals, a birthday party. The joy of Sunday worship quickly disappeared.

When the children saw me looking at the calendar they surmised it was time to push their particular agendas. A chorus of voices rang out.

"I need a new pair of tennis shoes. Can we go to Wal-Mart today?"

"Can Rebekah spend the night Friday?"

"You promised to take us to the lake. When are we going?"

Something snapped. "Be quiet!" I shouted. "Go back to your rooms and get your chores done...now!" Dead silence and hurt looks. *Dear Jesus,* I breathed. *Forgive my short temper. The needs of my children are overwhelming. I am so burdened. Please help me.* Suddenly a Bible reference came to mind and chided my turbulent spirit.

"Martha, Martha, you are worried and bothered about so many things: but only a few things are necessary, really only one. The part that Mary has chosen is best; and it shall not be taken away from her."[1] "Seek first His kingdom and His righteousness, and all these things shall be added to you."[2]

We must evaluate our priorities. Even good possessions and wholesome activities may not be important at the moment.

Charles E. Hummel wisely wrote: "It is not God who loads us until we bend or crack with an ulcer, nervous breakdown, heart attack, or stroke. These come from our inner compulsions, coupled with the pressure of circumstances." He warns against "letting the urgent things crowd out the important."[3] God gives us sufficient time to accomplish the work He has intended for our lives.

Martha of Bethany was frantically busy with what she perceived as important work while Mary sat at Jesus' feet. Mary had discerned what was important and was commended for it. Think about Jesus' words and Mary's example. Midst the frenzy of everyday life, are we doing what matters? In chasing our wants are we neglecting our children? In attempting to satisfy their wants, are we losing sight of their true needs?

Beyond a child's need for health and his mother's presence, what is critical for him? I suspect many essentials are neglected in modern life and that they don't cost extra money. They require gifts of time, love, and discipline.

The following discussion is not intended to be exhaustive, nor do I claim to be an ultimate authority on the subject. However, as Dr. Denmark has encouraged me, I would like to encourage every mom who reads this book to periodically reevaluate her own priorities and thoughtfully determine the individual needs of her children. It's usually best to avoid either comparing one's family with the neighbor's or consulting your child's desires. Instead, study him with a prayer for wisdom and look to scriptural principles to guide you in determining what is crucial to his well-being.

Isn't the essence of mothering to discern the true needs of our offspring and give of ourselves sacrificially to meet them? And could it be that while mothering we might discover our own true needs along the way?

My father had a wonderful way of responding to our requests when we asked for something. He'd suggest we study it for three weeks, then see whether we still wanted the item. Nine times out of ten, we lost interest. I think about the boys I used to go with. Oh, they were great, but what if I had married one of them! It would have wrecked my life! What if God gave us everything we prayed for? Some things we desire may not be good for us. We can't have everything we want.

If parents would just teach their children that everything has a price.... One of the most important phrases for them to learn is "I can't afford it." The happiest children in the world are those who have something to wish for, something to give them a thrill. But if they get everything they want, there's no thrill. I'll never forget what Mary said one day to a friend as they played outside my window. She was admiring the other child's pretty dress.

"Why don't you ask your mother to buy you one like it?" the little girl asked.

"We can't afford it," Mary answered. I was so glad to hear her say that. She learned as a child that there were things we couldn't afford, and she was content with what she had. I've never heard her complain about not having enough.

Back to the Basics

When Scripture promises "God shall supply all your needs according to His riches in glory in Christ Jesus,"[4] I don't believe it necessarily refers to a new car or a steak every Friday night. When addressing physical needs, it generally speaks of essentials in terms of food, clothing, and shelter.

There was a time when women took pride in doing a good job with the basics—clean clothes, a clean house, and nourishing food. We should find joy in the same.

Are you so busy with the extra curricular that your children live on fast or convenience foods. Are their sheets clean? Are they learning how to keep their rooms neat? Is your little girl's hair well brushed, and does your son need a haircut? Is your newborn getting enough quiet time? Does everyone dress for breakfast? (We're still working on this one.)

Some are more capable than others of juggling numerous activities while furnishing the basics. You must realistically evaluate your own capabilities and responsibilities and be at peace with the measure God has provided you. Finances, energy level, organizational skills, number and ages of children, husband's support, and many other factors influence whether we are a "one-or five-ring-circus" mom.

If the basics are sliding, you may need to eliminate other commitments. It's vital to the tranquillity of your home that you be content. Successfully managing family responsibilities is an accomplishment that shouldn't be minimized. All who do it deserve congratulations and encouragement. How quickly life can become chaotic and marriages strained when a mother is unable to handle her primary duties. I advise moms, especially those with young children, to be extremely hesitant about committing themselves to outside activities. If they want to do a good job at home, it's wise for them to minimize time spent in the car and in trivial conversations on the phone. Do I have to mention switching off the TV?

Time

Our generation has forgotten how to live. Trying desperately to grab the most of life, many of us have thrown our lives away.

We drag our children along at our frantic pace, anxious that they receive the best of all possible educational and social experiences.

Don't forget that children, particularly very young children, need time to ponder, to observe nature, and relax. Curling up in a corner with a book, eating and digesting food, asking questions of an attentive listener—all enhance their daily growth and take time. Slow down, mothers. Learn to enjoy simple pleasures like taking the kids for a walk in the neighborhood. Read them a good story; let them help or just watch while you make a special Friday-night dessert. Don't get stuck on the treadmill of overcommitting your finances or your time (a much more valuable commodity). In both cases it's enormously stressful. I write from personal experience. Keep in mind that investing unhurried time in the lives of your little ones will bring far greater returns than any monetary investment you can make.

In contrast to our frenzied existence stands the example of Christ. Charles Hummel observes: "His life was never feverish; He had time for people. He could spend hours talking to one person, such as the Samaritan woman at the well. His life showed wonderful balance..."[5]

If a little one says he's bored, don't assume he has too much time on his hands or that he needs additional stimulation from outside activities and/or sophisticated toys. Certainly don't turn on the television. Hand him a piece of paper and pencil or some paints. Give him a roll of masking tape and a cardboard box. Restlessness can be an excellent stimulus for creativity.

I don't remember my mother ever being in a hurry or raising her voice at any one of us. She never made us feel we were working her to death, and I never heard her say, "You children are wearing me out!"

How did she stay so patient with twelve children? I think if you had been in my office today, you'd wonder how I stay so calm. There were babies crying in both side rooms, mamas slapping and yelling. I could get awfully upset. I could lose my temper at the parents and say, "Don't come back if you won't follow my advice."

I think my mother handled it just the way I do; she had self control. If you don't have it, you'd better find some. If a mother raises her voice, the children will too. If she slaps, they will follow her example. Sometimes I'm asked, "Dr. Denmark, what makes my children so bad?"

"Go look in the mirror," I say, "You get apples off apple trees."

Extracurricular activities are great, but they shouldn't interfere with family relationships. I'm all for sports, but many children involved in them don't eat supper with the family. I knew one little girl whose activities almost wrecked her. She was taking violin, organ, and dancing lessons. That child never had a chance to play or have quiet times at home. She never had time to go into her room and be creative.

Everybody has time to do the things he wants to do. We need to psychoanalyze ourselves, asking, Is it that I don't have the time or that I don't want to take the time? Anything we have to do is work. Anything we want to do is play.

Patience, patience, patience...a mother needs to be so patient and to be a real diplomat, too. Everyone gives her advice. She should listen carefully, respectfully, to it all and then just do what she thinks is best.

Adolescents and Time

As much as young children need time for quietness, reflection, and creativity, so older children in the midst of hormonal changes need to be busy. Idleness is surely the devil's workshop when it comes to adolescents. Bad behavior during the teen years can cause permanent damage to a child's future. Much depression, frustration, immorality, and unhealthy introspection may be avoided if young adults are occupied with plenty of wholesome activities. Busy-ness doesn't have to be hectic but keep your young adults occupied with chores, challenging projects, sports, community service, inspiring books, and part-time employment. Help them follow their own interests and discover their individual strengths and weaknesses through work and responsibility.

There is no guarantee a child will turn out right no matter how wonderful his parents have been. There comes a time when he must make his own choices. However, if he has been brought up right, he has had a model to follow. He knows right from wrong.

There are times during adolescent years when a child rejects his upbringing no matter how wonderful his parents have been, but I believe the prodigal son came back because he remembered those clean white sheets and that good fried chicken.

Adolescence can be the most miserable period of one's life. Bodily changes occur so fast it's difficult to keep up with them, and an adolescent struggles with identity—he's neither child nor adult.

Sometimes adolescents talk with me, bemoaning the fact that girlfriends or boyfriends have taken up with others. I always say, "Be glad for them that they found someone. Be happy for them. Besides, it's likely another streetcar will come around the corner soon!"

"Don't do or say anything you'll regret later," I tell young people. "Once you've done or said something, you can never take it back. God can forgive, but you can't forget."

I encourage a young person to put a little note on his mirror which says something like this: "As long as I live in my parents' home, sleep in their bed, and eat their food, I will obey their rules. Some-day I'll have a son or daughter of my own, and I will want him to obey my rules."

The adolescent years are like those of a woman going through menopause. There are a lot of hormonal changes, but you have to go through it. If a woman can keep very busy during that period, leave off taking estrogen and all that mess women typically take during those changes, and stay out of doctors' offices, she would be better off. Eventually menopause will pass and she can settle down to being a nice old lady. When adolescents pass through their hormonal changes, they begin to settle down too.

Jacob Abbott's Wisdom

His book *Training Children in Godliness* was so helpful to me in evaluating priorities and planning my work that I have quoted several paragraphs from the chapter entitled "Teaching Children to Be Happy." The words of this nineteenth-century educator, minister, and author will never grow outdated.

"So whatever may be the reader's situation and condition in life, if he wishes to be happy, let him regulate his affairs. If you have uncertain, unsettled accounts open, which you have been dreading to examine, go and explore the cases thoroughly and have them closed. If there are plans which you have been intending to accomplish, but which you have been postponing, summon your resolution and carry them at once into effect, or else determine to abandon them and dismiss them from your thoughts.

"The mind of young and ardent man becomes loaded with crude, half-formed designs, unfinished plans, and duties postponed. He is like a child unaccustomed to the world, who takes a walk on a pleasant summer's day. Every object seems valuable, and he picks up a pebble here, a stick there, and gathers a load of pretty flowers in this place and that, until he becomes so encumbered with his treasures that he can hardly go on. They are constantly slipping and dropping from his hands, and become a source of perplexity and anxiety to him because he cannot retain them all. So it is with us. Every plan which reason forms or imagination paints, we think we must execute; but after having made a new beginning, a new project which we are equally eager to secure enters our heads. In a short time, we become encumbered with a mass of intellectual lumber which we cannot carry and are unwilling to leave. Consider what you can and will execute, and take hold of the execution of them now. Abandon the rest, so that you may move forward with a mind that is free and uncluttered.

"This, then, is the second great rule for securing personal happiness. Look over your affairs, and arrange and methodize everything. Define in your own mind what you have to do, and dismiss everything else. Take time for reflection, and plan all your work so as to go on smoothly and quietly so that the mind may be ahead of all its duties, choosing its own way, and going forward in peace.

"There is one point in connection with this subject of the management of worldly affairs which should not be passed by, and which is yet an indispensable condition of human happiness. I mean the duty of every man to bring his expenses and his financial liabilities fairly within his control. There are some cases of a peculiar character, and some occasional emergencies, perhaps, in the life of every person, which constitute exceptions; but this is the general rule.

"Reduce your expenditures, your style of living, and your business far below your financial means, so that you may have money in plenty.... Almost all are eagerly reaching forward to a station in life a little above what they can well afford, or struggling to do a business a little more extensive than they have capital or steady credit for. Thus all through life they keep just above their means; and just above, by even a small excess, is inevitable misery.

"If your aim is happiness, reduce your style of living and your responsibilities of business to such a point that you shall easily be able to reach it. Do this, I say, at all costs.... For there is such a thing as happiness in a single room, with plain furniture and simple fare; but there is no such thing as happiness, with responsibilities which cannot be met and debts increasing, without any prospect of their discharge. If your object is power, the credit of belonging to good society, or the most rapid accumulation of property, and you are willing to sacrifice happiness for it, I might perhaps give you different advice. But if your object is happiness, then this is the only way."[6]

TLC

Mothering is an art requiring great sensitivity, perseverance, and wisdom. There are many balances to maintain as a mom nurtures her child. Family life and routine shouldn't revolve around a child's desires, or he will grow to be a tyrant and seldom content. He may never fully adjust to the reality that he isn't the center of the universe. There are many simple ways to build emotional security without raising a tyrant.

Take the following inventory: Am I establishing eye contact with my child? Am I listening carefully to his words? Do I take time to answer questions thoughtfully (not necessarily every question)? Do I examine his handiwork seriously? Do I share in the joy of his accomplishments and sympathize with his sorrows?

Stop occasionally and do something that's fun with your child, even if it's very simple. I think with fondness of the time my grandmother mended my dress and sewed on a button for me. Together we searched through her button tin for one that matched. She let me choose. We took our time, and she even let me thread the needle—wow! I remember those beautiful buttons, my grandmother's smile and gentle hands! But, I especially cherish how comfortable and loved I felt sitting close beside Mama Lois while she listened to my prattle and sewed for me.

Dr. Denmark is a great example of one who gives TLC even in the midst of her busy schedule. On winter days she usually has a space heater in her office. After examining my children, she warms their clothes in front of it before I redress them. This simple but thoughtful act makes little ones feel special. Thank you, Dr. D.!

Boundaries

A child needs boundaries in his play area and in his behavior. Just as a fence in the back yard provides physical safety, so behavioral boundaries bring emotional security. Children are confused and frustrated when allowed to do one thing one day and disallowed the next. It is up to the parents (with God's guidance) to establish limits and enforce them consistently. Expectations should be spelled out as well as the penalties for violating a rule.

Do you want your child to pick up his clothes after bathing? He must be required to do so until the habit is firmly established. If he doesn't follow through, reasonable penalties are necessary. Do you want him to speak respectfully to adults? Teach him specifically what that means and insist that he comply.

Anything you start with little people you have to keep up. Perform an action three times, and they will expect it to be repeated. "Consistency" should be written on every wall of your home.

Teamwork

A family should learn to function as a team. Scripture says: "Two are better than one because they have a good return for their labor. For if either of them falls, the one will lift up his companion."[7] A team does much better than one alone. If one of its members is ailing, others are there to pitch in.

Many of today's children view their parents as facilitators. Mom and Dad exist to provide the money and transportation necessary to fulfill their wants. In contrast, let's train our children to see themselves as part of a cooperative effort, working toward accomplishing God-given family goals. They need to see their responsibility toward their family, not just to themselves. Teamwork means working together and taking turns. Chores should be shared among all according to ability. Naturally, older members have the most responsibility, but no one should be unfairly burdened with work.

If sister is sick other siblings ought to take up the slack and cheerfully help with her chores because their turn will come. Does brother have a special event coming up? Sister should be willing to baby-sit while mother takes him shopping for a new shirt. Instead of being jealous, everyone can be proud of him when he sings his solo. Was baby born with a physical handicap? The whole family ought to view him as their corporate responsibility to encourage, give therapy, and help with his special challenge.

Numerous examples illustrate that kind of cooperation. The sooner parents inculcate the concept in their children the better.

Even two-year-old Joseph can help six-year-old Esther set the table by placing the napkins. The younger a child understands he's part of a team effort, the less likely he is to resent chores and responsibilities. "Many willing hands make light and joyous work!" It's a great old saying!

Ministry

To fully appreciate our own circumstances, all of us need to broaden our perspectives to include those outside our own families, particularly these less fortunate than we who may need us. We have a natural tendency to become self-centered and feed that self centeredness in our children by focusing exclusively on their needs and desires.

Involve your children, especially the older ones, in serving others. Most church communities provide plenty of opportunity— phone calling, collecting clothes for a crisis pregnancy outreach, baby-sitting for a sidewalk counselor, visiting a neglected senior citizen, helping cook a meal or cleaning for a new mother, using their pennies to sponsor a child overseas, working in a soup kitchen.

Children can help fill some very real needs, and it's excellent for their growth in character to be involved outside the home. A word of caution is needed: it usually means extra time on the road for their mothers. As important as these ministries are, be realistic in evaluating the time required for them. Don't become so overburdened that essential household chores are neglected. Your ministry to your home is vital and mustn't be sacrificed for any extended period of time. Maybe Daddy can help with the chauffeuring!

Direction

Many children possess a beguiling sense of confidence in their own discretion. They are certain they know what they need and what's best for them. If you're at all insecure in your own judgment, their confident assertions can easily sway you. Children are masters at lobbying for their own agendas. In truth, most children have very little discernment as to what is best for them. Did your fourteen-year-old really have to stay up till midnight? Did Suzie need that bag of candy?

Children require direction from parents who model disciplined lives and study their true needs. Parents shouldn't allow themselves to be guilt-manipulated by them or by other parents. They, themselves, ought to be the source of direction. "This food is what's best for your body...that activity is bad for your spiritual growth...no, we are not going to watch that movie."

Everyone knows a good example is the best teacher. No one is perfect. Be honest about your inconsistencies, but try to instruct by word and deed. Your children need it more than they will ever admit.

Suppose someone brought a stranger to Atlanta, letting him off at Five Points with no maps or directions, and told him to find his way home. Which road would he take? There are a dozen intersections there offering a hundred ways he might go.

If a child knows where home is, he'll have no problem, but most children don't. My mother kept me home for eight years. I was a Daughtry. I knew the Daughtry way of life; I knew the way home. Had my early childhood been spent in a daycare center, I would have seen many different ways of life. A little fellow in day care is in the middle of the city and doesn't know how to get home.

Our streets and jails are full of people who have grown up without parental guidance. I've worked in the slums since 1918, and so many of them say the same thing: "When I was a child, my parents didn't help me, didn't feed me. They had plenty of money but no time for me."

Once a man asked me to "straighten out" his three wayward children. The mother's teeth were so brown from tobacco stains that when she smiled her mouth looked like a dark hole. The father looked even worse. I thought to myself, If I had a stallion that looked like that man and a mare that looked like that mother, I wouldn't expect their colt to be a Kentucky race horse.

Dreams

Children need to dream, to have something to yearn for. They love birthday parties and special events. Half the joy is in the anticipation. If birthday parties came every day, they would soon be old hat. Don't fulfill your children's wants instantly. Give them something to work for. Teach them to wait and anticipate.

Your daughter wants a new dress? Help her sew one. Your son wants a toy car? Tell him he might get it for Christmas. Maybe if he does some extra chores around the house, he can earn enough to purchase it himself.

Encourage your children to look forward to the future. What would they like to accomplish with their lives? What would they like to save their pennies for? Help them take the first steps toward fulfilling those goals. It's depressing to look around and observe moral and economic decline in our culture. There's reason for discouragement and even outrage, Yet in our pessimism let's not rob our children of their hopes. Children need dreams.

Christmas was a great time for us because we received gifts that were special, things we normally didn't get, except once a year. There was an orange, nuts, raisins, toys, a doll perhaps. It was a thrill, but now a child is bought a new toy with every trip to the store. Where is the thrill? It's kind of like...well, modern marriage. If a couple's been living together before the wedding, what's the point in a honeymoon?

When I was eight years old and went off to school for the first time, it was really exciting. Our parents gave me a pencil box and a little book satchel. It was a thrill to go to school. Children nowadays have been in institutions since they were six weeks old. There are no thrills for little kids anymore.

Children should learn to want something. Now there's no incentive to make a toy; they just go to the store and buy it. They don't have to read a book—just turn on the TV.

Christ

The New Testament tells us about a time when the Jewish mothers brought their children to Jesus to be blessed.[8] His disciples rebuked them, probably thinking He was too busy with other more important matters to be bothered with children. But Jesus was indignant and intervened. He was never too busy for little ones. He took them in his arms, blessed them and said, "The kingdom of God belongs to such as these."[9] What a tender, wonderful story. What an encouragement to those mothers.

Are we willing to follow their example in bringing our children to Christ? Do we pray for them and show them the person of Christ as he is presented in the Bible? What about taking them to church to gain true knowledge of the Savior? They need

Christ above all else so they will understand the nature of sin, forgiveness, and grace. None of us (children included) is innocent. We must reconcile with our Creator, and that can only be done through Christ.

Children need to understand life as God intended it to be, learning to see it through the "spectacles" of Scripture. Teach them to study the Bible and to solve problems and find answers according to the principles found in God's Word.

We normally study and memorize Scripture after breakfast while everyone is still seated at the table. Scripture memory is followed by prayer with the children taking turns depending on which day of the week it is. (David prays on Monday, Esther on Tuesday, etc.) After supper we read a good Bible story book, sing, and close with prayer again. This simple routine keeps us consistent. My favorite Bible study aids are: *The Child's Story Bible* by Catherine F. Vos; *Leading Little Ones to God* by Marian M. Schoolland; the *Child's Catechism* (younger children) and the *Shorter Catechism* (older children). The catechisms are a wonderful summary of the teachings of the Bible. We study and memorize the question and answers.

The essence of mothering is to discern the important, the true needs of our children and give of ourselves sacrificially to meet them. The wisest mother comes to God for that discernment. Surely the one who made your children knows what they need.

Bring your children to Jesus. At his feet, they will discover the important things, the "best part," as Mary of Bethany did long ago.

Notes

1. Luke 10:42 (New English Bible)
2. Luke 6:33
3. Charles Hummel, *Tyranny of the Urgent* (Downers Grove, IL: InterVarsity Press), 1967.
4. Philippians 4:19
5. Hummel, *Tyranny of the Urgent.*
6. Jacob Abbott, *Training Children in Godliness*, ed. Michael J. McHugh (Arlington Heights, IL: Christian Library Press, 1992), 114–16.
7. Ecclesiastes 4:9-10
8. Mark 10:14–16; Matthew 19:13–15; Luke 18:15–17
9. Mark 10:14

Vaccinations

One of Dr. Leila Denmark's greatest accomplishments was her work over an eleven-year period on the vaccine for pertussis. She received the 1935 Fisher Award for outstanding research in diagnosis, treatment, and immunization of whooping cough.

In light of modern controversy over routine vaccinations, the following interview with Dr. Denmark is especially relevant. Her perspective on how they should be administered is based on extensive experience beginning with that research and extending to the present. Because of the longevity of her practice, she has probably vaccinated more children than any one physician in the world today.

Q. "Dr. Denmark, one of the greatest accomplishments of your life has been the vital part you played in developing the pertussis vaccine. I understand it's the same one given routinely to infants in DPT shots (the P in DPT standing for pertussis). Will you trace for us the history of how you developed it and what prompted your work?"

A. "In 1932 I saw about three lines in the *Journal of the American Medical Association* saying that some doctor was speculating about a possible vaccine for whooping cough. His name was Sauer. At that time I had an enormous group of kids sick with it at Central Presbyterian Church Baby Clinic. I had lost triplets at Grady Hospital. I had

twins with intercranial hemorrhages and a world of patients losing all
their meals and having seizures every four hours. Something had to be
done. At that time I heard of a man in East Point who had it and had
fractured two ribs and hemorrhaged in his eyes from coughing. I went
to his house and asked if he would let me have some of his blood (I
wouldn't do that today because that would be "terrible"). I took 100
cc.'s and put it in the icebox. The next morning I took the serum off
and injected a child subcutureously with it. It cured him like magic.
Then I knew there was something we could do.

"One of the most interesting things I discovered at that time was
that I could use a mother's blood to cure her sick baby if she had had
whooping cough herself. If a nursing baby had been sick for about a
week, I took 100 cc.'s of his mother's blood, took the serum off, and
put it in subcutaneously. The antibody response was just as good as
when I used the East Point man's blood. Of course that, too, was terrible. Today we're afraid of AIDS. I'd be put in jail. But I proved my
point...there was something we could do to help these children.

"Understand, if a patient has suffered whooping cough for the
full six weeks, the disease runs its course and he is immune for life.
However, if the disease is cured through antibiotics or serum, the
patient doesn't develop permanent immunity because he hasn't built
up enough antibodies. I realized we needed an effective vaccine, so
I wrote Eli Lilly Company to ask them if they would make one I
could test...like Dr. Sauer's. I did hundreds of vaccinations with it
and all kinds of blood tests to determine the level of immunity that
developed. I ended up using a complement fixation test to determine
immunity. I gave those kids the vaccine that Lilly sent me. About 25
percent of them showed a 4+ on the complement fixation. It wasn't
enough, so I asked Lilly to double the strength. I found we did far
better with that. Two more times I asked them to double it again
and found that 99 percent of those children got the same antibody
response they would have from a full case of the disease. They were

immune. But I didn't do the research all by myself—Eli Lilly, Cutter, Emory Public Health Department, and a lot of other people helped.

"For many years I continued taking serum from my vaccinated children and sending it to the two drug companies to test for immunity. Then I found a very interesting procedure called an agglutination test. I took a drop of blood from a child's finger and put it with the antigen. In a minute I could determine whether the vaccinations had effectively immunized the child."

Q. "Didn't you use this same test up until a few years ago? I believe you tested my oldest daughter after her DPTs."

A. "That's right. But Lilly quit making the vaccine, and I couldn't get the antigen. Cutter made me some, but it didn't work. So a few years ago, I quit testing my patients for an antibody response."

Q. "Did you do research on when the vaccine should be administered?"

A. "Yes, and I found out something that was critical. I began by vaccinating a pregnant mother, thinking I could immunize the baby inside her. The antibody response was no good. After birth, when the baby was a month old, I gave him a shot, but it didn't work; at two months it didn't work and so on. I began to get a wonderful response about the fifth month. I discovered that until then the child's immune system isn't mature enough to respond effectively."

Q. "Some now say the pertussis vaccine can cause dangerous reactions like encephalitis, seizures, convulsions, fever up to 106°, and breathing problems. They even accuse it of causing **Sudden Infant Death Syndrome** (SIDS or crib death). How do you feel about such allegations?"

A. "They're big lies! I've been using it since 1932 without ever encountering a severe reaction from it. I wouldn't pay any attention to such propaganda. There is always somebody tearing down things we try to do."

Q. "So you think the DPT vaccine is as good now as it was years ago?"

A. "That's right, but if it's given too early, it doesn't do any good. Sometimes they give it to sick kids and then blame the vaccine for the illness. I always give it in the deltoid muscle, not in the fat of the leg.

"I remember doing research down at McDonough, Georgia. A child had had the shots and was rumored to be paralyzed because of them. I had to investigate and asked the mother, 'How old was the baby when he held his head up?' He never had. 'How old was he when he turned over in bed?' He never had. They had been blaming his immobility on the vaccine, not realizing he had *amyotonia congentia*. There are so many cases like that. If they'd really study this thing, they would know there's nothing wrong with the vaccine.

"I could send a child to the hospital to get his tonsils out, and the next morning he might wake with a 106 degree temperature and break out with the measles. Some would say, 'Never take out tonsils because tonsillectomies cause measles.' During a polio epidemic, a doctor in Cincinnati took a baby's tonsils out. The next morning the baby was paralyzed. Some said, 'Don't ever take tonsils out, the tonsillectomy paralyzed the child.' The child already had polio, but no one knew it. It's so easy to blame vaccinations for a concurrent condition. I wish people who say these things could just go back and see what it was like before. Vaccines are the greatest thing that ever happened for little children."

Q. "About **Sudden Infant Death Syndrome**. There is so much talk today about SIDS. Would you say a few words about it?"

A. "I've been practicing medicine for almost seventy years, and I've never had a SIDS baby because I insist that mothers place their infants on their stomachs and instruct them how to make the baby's bed correctly (see pages 12–13).

"There are a lot of things that might make a baby die. A baby with meningitis can die in his sleep. But I don't believe an infant can get what we call SIDS unless he is placed on his back. I know I'm right. An infant on its back is in constant danger of asphyxiating on its own spit up. The child may burp up a mouth full of milk and breathe it into his lungs, choking himself to death. It only takes a little thing to choke an infant to death.

"A man received a grant to study SIDS and did a lot of his research in countries where babies sleep on sheepskins. I can imagine one might smother if he was placed on his stomach with his face buried in thick wool. That particular researcher concluded an infant should always be place on his back or side. Placing a baby on its back is potentially fatal. On his side he may not get SIDS, but he's unable to exercise his muscles properly and gets his little head out of shape. Babies need to use all four limbs and the muscles in their necks. They can't do that unless they are on their stomachs.

"I had a patient in here not long ago who was about four months old and had been put in one of those devices that kept him propped on his side. Four months old and he couldn't hold his head up because he had never used the muscles in his neck! His right arm was weak and the side of his head was very flat.

"A baby placed on his stomach feels secure. He spits up onto the crib sheet without danger, can exercise his muscles well, and develops a nicely shaped head. It is so important."

Q. "What's the worst reaction a patient is likely to get from a DPT shot?"

A. "Four hours later there may be a little fever that lasts about twelve hours, but nothing more than that. Aspirin takes care of it.

We used to give pertussis separately. It never caused a fever, but there was a little from the diphtheria and tetanus. So the temperature was from them, not the pertussis."

Q. "With actual whooping cough, you don't usually get fever."
A. "Not unless there is a secondary infection."

Q. "But with diphtheria and tetanus (the diseases), you do get fever."
A. "Oh, boy, you sure do!"

Q. "Have any of your fully inoculated patients ever contracted whooping cough?"
A. "Never. If you are vaccinated correctly, you'll never have it, and I don't believe you need more than those three DPT shots. Some of my former patients were vaccinated sixty two years ago and never got it. My own daughter, Mary, is an example."

Q. "What if a child has only a single DPT?"
A. "It take three DPT shots to be fully immunized. I believe I had used the vaccines separately for about eleven years, then Dr. Kendrick put the DPT together. I did it about a week apart back then, but you could conceivably give them once a year until the series was completed. On the other hand, I believe you could give the shots once a day and it wouldn't harm the patient. They are normally given a month apart."

Q. "Many people are concerned about giving a triple vaccination because the child's immune system is required to fight three toxins simultaneously rather than individually."
A. "Oh, that's ridiculous! Some say you can't eat proteins and starches in the same day. So you eat the meat one day and the

vegetables the next. But the stomach has all kinds of enzymes and digestive juices to digest anything all the time. The body can incur three diseases at the same time and heal itself from them simultaneously, so we can also handle three vaccinations at once."

Q. "According to antivaccine sources, the effects are potentially more severe than the disease itself. They claim the vaccines can be contaminated with animal viruses. Some point out that the chemical makeup of the vaccines is different and thereby potentially more dangerous than the actual disease. Certain researches claim that injecting them directly into the body messes up the immune system and prevents it from responding effectively."

A. "I have just one answer to all that. From my many years of experience I find none of that is true."

Q. "Some researchers claim that diphtheria, pertussis, and tetanus were already on the decline before the vaccinations were introduced, that the DPTs did not actually contribute to the decrease of these illnesses."

A. "Well, I think those researchers ought to go back to about 1932 or 1933 and see what things were like then. At that time, I had seventy-five cases of whooping cough at Central Presbyterian Clinic. We were having diphtheria, tetanus, and polio too. None of those diseases were declining on their own, but now we have vaccines that stop them from happening."

Q. "How would you respond to those who insist that a significant percentage of cases were actually caused by the vaccines?"

A. "Oh, that's a farce."

Q. "If cases are now rare, why bother inoculating?"

A. "They're rare because most children, except some of the

very poor, receive the vaccine. I had one family that didn't believe in it until the father happened to get whooping cough. He was terribly sick. Their five-month-old baby got it, too, and probably would have died without erythromycin. If you spoke to that daddy today, he would tell you whooping cough is still bad. He's become a convert who believes in the vaccine."

Q. "If people stopped getting it, the disease would increase again. Is this right?"

A. "We'd be right back to where we were, oh yes! We think we've completely eliminated smallpox because they've used the vaccine in all countries, so there's no more around. There hasn't even been any vaccine available for seven years. If someone came into the United States with smallpox, a lot of people would get it, but they wouldn't die the way they used to because we have antibiotics. People don't have to get secondary infections. For whooping cough, we've got chloromycetin or erythromycin. Both can cure it."

Q. "I've heard that there haven't been any recent cases of smallpox. Is that right?"

A. "Yes, and I don't think we're having any big measles now either."

Q. "But you're saying that there are enough cases of DPT that we need to keep vaccinating."

A. "Sure. The government has furnished vaccines for years but there are a lot of poor people who have no way to go get it. Some people just don't bother. We still find the diseases, especially in the slums."

Q. "Do you think most mothers and perhaps doctors of my generation really understand the horror of such diseases?"

A. "Oh, no, I don't think so at all. They haven't seen little kids coughing for six weeks, having seizures every four hours, vomiting with each cough, unable to retain fluids. The horrible things they had to go through! They were choking to death, and you were beating their backs trying to get them to breathe again. A child with diphtheria can't breathe at all. You have to put a tube in his neck. A child with polio can't walk. They say war is hell, but I can't fully comprehend the horror of war because I've never been in one. If people had to experience these dreadful illnesses, they'd have an entirely different opinion."

Q. "Is there a difference between the effectiveness of the killed-virus polio vaccine and the live-virus (oral) version ?"
A. "I don't see any."

Q. "What about the MMR (measles, mumps, and rubella) vaccination? Is it important?"
A. "Very! I know the measles part works, but I'm not so sure about the other two. I've had vaccinated patients who developed both, but not measles."

Q. "There are researchers who claim that incurring those childhood illnesses actually strengthens a child's immune system. Do you agree?"
A. "One does become immune by going through them, but they can impair one's health. The vaccine is just as strengthening to the immune system as having the disease, but there's no suffering. The diseases do lots of bad things to your body that vaccine doesn't—it's such a simple, easy way of avoiding illness."

Q. "What about flu shots?"
A. "I believe all flu is caused by H Influenza, a definite organ-

ism. In 1940 I had somebody make me a vaccine with H Influenza organisms, but I didn't use it as we do today. I started with a tenth of a cc. and increased one-tenth each visit for twelve shots, but the kids still got the flu. I'm a hundred years old, and I suppose I've had it a hundred times. If you can't immunize by having a disease, there is no way you make an effective vaccine. You can't immunize against strep and staph either."

Q. "Do you think that having it done each year can immunize you for that one particular year?"

A. "No, I don't think it does a thing. You can have flu three times in one winter. I don't think you can immunize against H influenza any more than you can against strep, or staph or pneumcoccus which causes pneumonia."

Q. "What do you think of the newer vaccinations such as the HIb for spinal meningitis and hepatitis B now given to newborns in hospitals?"

A. "The HIb is similar to the influenza shot; I don't think it works. I used the flu shot for years, and it didn't seem to do any good. But I'm not going to criticize anybody's vaccine for the simple reason that when I was researching mine, I knew that I had to find a way to prove it. And these people have to test it. Now, I've never had a case of hepatitis in my practice. I don't believe the vaccine hurts, but I don't know whether it helps. That's the point."

Q. "Are there any vaccinations you're opposed to or consider even slightly dangerous?"

A. "No. Immunizations and baby food are the greatest things that have ever happened on this earth for little people." (For further information on immunizations see pages 29–30.)

Storytime

In the foyer of Dr. Denmark's office is a screen plastered with pictures of her patients. There must be hundreds of smiling little faces representing only a fraction of the lives Dr. Denmark has touched during her seventy-five years of practice. I love looking at the photos: fat-cheeked cherubs, snaggle-toothed ballerinas; an Olan Mills Christmas shot with junior dressed in his red vest. If one looks closely enough one can find a Bowman or two.

I often think each picture represents a story of the impact a faithful physician has on the life of a family. Each story is a tiny thread in a beautiful tapestry of one life spent serving others. I've heard many of them and want to share a few with you.

Generations

Dr. Denmark may never know much she means to me and my family. Before I had a child, my husband's grandmother spoke of the wonderful doctor to whom she had taken her three children. My mother-in-law in turn had taken hers there. They both mentioned how she made managing children and home so natural, what a great person she is, and how just knowing her enriched their lives. Of course, it was Dr. Denmark.

When my own daughter was born it would have been only natural to do the same, but I wasn't quite smart enough to follow their advice immediately. I selected a doctor a little nearer home, thinking all pediatricians were alike. Virginia was a beautiful, healthy baby, and before she was born I had decided to nurse her. It worked pretty well at first, but she soon started fussing about an hour after feeding. The problem grew worse until she was crying constantly. The doctor diagnosed her with reflux and eventually prescribed Zantac to be given after feedings. When she was four months old we were to go on our first out-of-town trip. Totally exasperated with her crying all morning, I kept asking myself how I would be able to deal with it in a small car for three hours. Almost as an answered prayer, the thought came: take her to Dr. Denmark. I put my sweet, pitiful baby in the car and went directly to the miracle worker I had heard so much about. It was a busy day for the good doctor, so we had to wait a while. But my nerves calmed as we sat watching the happy, well-behaved children in her care. I just knew she would have an answer to my precious child's problem.

Dr. Denmark asked a few brief questions as she examined Virginia.

"Was she nursed or bottle fed?" I had stopped producing milk and was feeding her formula. "How much was she taking at a time?" I'd been told to give her six ounces of milk at a feeding. "What else is she getting?" They hadn't even mentioned other food yet. She looked at me and said, "This child is starving. She should be getting eight ounces of milk and protein, vegetables, fruit, and a starch." I was horrified. Here I lived amid abundance, and my innocent baby was starving! I was ashamed. I loved my child and wanted the very best for her, yet I wasn't even feeding her enough. Dr. Denmark smiled.

"I think we can save her," she said. She sat me down and gave me a list of what Virginia should eat. She also explained how to prepare her meals and maintain a common-sense schedule.

I went straight home, threw away the expensive medicine, and fed her as instructed. Then we left to see my parents for the weekend. Her proud grandparents were amazed at how well she ate. Her mood was better, and she went straight to sleep that night instead of crying until one or two o'clock in the morning.

At this writing Virginia is sixteen months old. I have taken her only to Dr. Denmark since that day. She is happy, goes to bed on schedule, and sleeps well. Everything my husband's grandmother and mother told me about raising a child under Dr. Denmark's care I have found to be absolutely true. People say that I am lucky to have such a wonderful daughter. Lucky? I don't think so. God sent us Virginia, but we are blessed to know Dr. Leila Daughtry Denmark and benefit from her vast knowledge and experience.

—Denise Garner Jacob
Alpharetta, Georgia

Dr. Denmark has always been an angel in my life. Not only has she cared for my children for fifteen years but was my own pediatrician too. When I first took the children to her, Brooke was five, and I had recently had twin daughters. I was disillusioned with the medical profession, having gone through five years of high bills accumulated from scores of visits, not to mention prescriptions. I've never been a believer in dosing my family with drugs for every ache or pain. I knew Brooke's surface problems must stem from a bigger root problem and wanted to find out what it was. That was when someone told me I should go to Dr. Denmark.

I was surprised to learn she was still active, but I packed a lunch and some picture books, and we went to see a friendly face from my past. She's ageless!, I thought when I saw her. Could it be that she's wearing the same uniform? My thoughts were quickly redirected as she began to examine the children. The twins were put on her infamous "green mush" of beans, cereal, and bananas, pureed and fed twice a day—cereal and fruit mush at breakfast, only water to drink, and absolutely nothing between meals.

Next it was Brooke's turn. It was *deja vu* as I saw my daughter climb onto the tall wooden examining table where I used to sit. As she began her examination, Dr. Denmark talked with Brooke in a sweet and personable way, her comments always carrying a positive word of encouragement.

"This is such a fine young lady. I don't think I'd sell her." Brooke and I watched and listened in awe. After a thorough going-over, from blood work to feeling the skin on her back and closely checking her hair, she looked at me and asked if anyone had ever told me Brooke was allergic to milk.

"No, never," I said as I thought of all the milk I poured into her daily.

"Let me tell you what you've been going through with this child," she said. As if actually experiencing it, she spoke of the ear infections, rounds of antibiotics, and head colds Brooke had suffered for the past five years.

"She probably has tubes in her ears," she added. Everything she named was right on course. Then she sat me down and began spelling it all out. With her hemoglobin at sixty, Brooke was anemic. "Most doctors won't tell you that isn't normal, but it's not. Everyone's hemoglobin should be at one hundred. You'll never be any healthier than your hemoglobin is high. If you do what I say we can get these children well. If you don't, then don't tell anyone I'm your doctor," she said. I can hear those words as if it were yesterday. No one had ever spoken to me in such a firm yet loving way. I knew she genuinely cared. She began explaining how the digestive system works, talking about her great dislike for milk and blaming it for the anemia among so many children.

"Not even animals go back on milk after they're weaned," she remarked. "But humans do. It takes at least two weeks to get milk out of one's system and that includes all dairy products." I should have been taking notes. I asked her if she wanted us to come back in two weeks.

"No," she said, "if you do what I say, you won't need to. And if not, then don't waste your time or mine." With that I knew she meant business. She indeed wanted to see my children happy and healthier, and I appreciated her candor. On the way home, I remembered how she used to tell my mother to feed us black-eyed peas and cabbage. Best food on earth. And boy! did Mother obey. I think we had black-eyed peas and cabbage at least once a week forever. Mother didn't let us eat between meals either. Well, it worked for me, so it would work for my children. We were about to make some lifestyle changes. Brooke's skin cleared up as did her congestion. Basically the girls' health has improved to the point that about all they need now is a yearly check-up.

—Jan Holland
Marietta, Georgia

With Love

Dr. Denmark has been an incredible mentor, doctor, and friend to all of my family! My twins, Preston and Jack, appeared on NBC television with her back in 1989 when they were a year old.

She has helped so much with my daughter. When Natalie was an infant, my husband and I took her to see Dr. Denmark because of a feeding problem, though we had been on her schedule from day one. She told us she would like to watch Natalie eat. Shortly afterward, she threw up all over the floor. I hurried to hand her to Joe so I could clean up the mess. Well, Dr. Denmark wouldn't hear of it. She insisted on getting down on her hands and knees and doing it herself—at ninety years old! She insisted I sit with my sweet baby. She has told me many times, "There is no more beautiful picture in all the world than a happy baby with its mother. There is no more pure love in the world than that." Well, maybe not I usually don't argue with Dr. Denmark. The love she gives to all her patients and their families comes mighty close!

—Liz May
Watkinsville, Georgia

Dr. Denmark is a remarkable woman. I began going to her when my daughter was three. Mollie had a chronic ear infection and was scheduled to have tubes put into her ears. My husband and I were uncomfortable at the idea and decided to try Dr. Denmark as a last resort.

"She has the kind of ears they like to put tubes in; don't let them! We'll give her antibiotics round the clock for seventy-two hours, and she'll be well," she said after one look. She didn't know why we were there—she just discovered the problem during a general exam. Mollie never had a recurrence!

Not only is Dr. Denmark the finest pediatrician I know, but she has shown us the kind of love and devotion that's hard to find. In January 1994 I called her in a panic because seven month-old R.J. was constipated and in extreme pain. She told me to immediately go to the children's emergency room. In very serious condition my son was diagnosed with Hirschbrung's disease and treated. They suggested surgery be considered to correct it, but we should try medical maintenance for a few months first. R.J. did fine for about six weeks then started having problems because his immune system was weakened. Three times in one month I had to call Dr. Denmark on her day off. All three times she had us come in and meet her at the office. When I told her the first time what had happened her reply astonished me.

"I am so relieved to see him," she said. "For weeks I've been wondering about and praying for a child with this condition, whoever it was." She really believed R.J. would overcome the disease if we stuck with the program he was on. So far, it's working well.

I truly believe God put Dr. Denmark on earth to not only heal children and educate parents but also to encourage mothers in their line of duty. She has lifted me up and made me feel that what I am doing is the greatest "job" I could ever have. How right she is.

—Nancy Eldredge
Lithia Springs, Georgia

Reprieve

At three months, my John Matthew had colic so badly he got no sleep day or night. He screamed and threw up everything he'd ingested. Dr. Denmark put him on a variety of solid foods along with cooked oatmeal, and the food stayed down. He was a different baby! After seeing numerous pediatricians with no help except the hollow words, "He'll outgrow it," I was so relieved. I'll never forget her wise words and gentle nature.

—Nancy Pyle
Roswell, Georgia

It was back in 1988 that I first heard about Leila Denmark from a gas station attendant. He had asked if my two -week-old in the car seat beside me had been sleeping through the night. I looked at him, puzzled, wondering how anyone could ask such a crazy question. As a first-time mother I was beyond exhausted. Cameron had been getting me up countless times at night ever since I brought him home. I thought it was normal. How could a baby sleep through the night? Well, the attendant's nine kids had all done so after their third night home. He said Dr. Denmark had the solution.

"Where is this woman?" I asked. He gave me directions, and I went the very next day, taking a pregnant friend with me. We found the humble office with a sign on the door saying "Closed Thursdays." But I had to see her! Maybe I should come back the next day...but how could I survive another night! I saw a big white house next door that was probably hers. She must have seen the desperation on my face when I knocked on the door.

"Let's go have a look at your baby," she said. We walked over to her office, and God gave me two hours with that wise woman. How I wished for a tape recorder. Her words were full of such simple common sense. It seems we make life so complicated for ourselves, but Dr. Denmark speaks of what matters in life and how important these little lives are. She is remarkable.

"Put the baby to bed, making sure he's fed and changed and burped. Then make sure there isn't a snake in his crib and leave: meaning leave him alone. Let him cry; it's good for him." Wit and wisdom, what a mix.

"What can I do that's good for my pregnancy?" my friend asked.

"Laugh a lot," Dr. Denmark replied. For a two-hour consultation the bill was eight dollars. After being with this special lady, you know she is one of God's gifts to our children.

—Leigh Smith Mintz
Roswell, Georgia

Before taking my first baby to Dr. Denmark I had been nursing her on demand and allowing her to sleep when she would. If she cried for more than five minutes, I picked her up to comfort her. By the time she was three months old my nerves were shattered from lack of sleep, my husband was wondering if he would ever have a meal and clean clothes again, and I was feeling desperate.

Dr. Denmark had me put my daughter on a schedule, assuring me that it was not only all right to let her cry but that it was actually good for her. Crying helps clean out the nose and strengthens the lungs.

Within a week, we had a much happier home. The baby and I were both sleeping all night. My outlook improved. I was no longer "leaking" through the night. I was soon able to prepare good, balanced meals for us all using Dr. Denmark's schedule as a guideline. It was comforting to know that what I fed my family would be building healthier bodies. With my once-colicky baby contentedly in her playpen, Mommy was able to catch up on the housework.

—Nora Dolberry Pitts
Dallas, Georgia

Answers

I am the mother of three girls and three boys and met Dr. Denmark when my third child was ten months old. A friend of mine heard him wheezing one day and suggested I see Dr. Denmark.

At the time of my first visit in 1989, he was anemic, and had ear and gastrointestinal infections. She said he probably had asthma that he would outgrow when he was five to nine years old, and that has held true for him. She told me to throw away the bottle and baby formula, start him on her diet, and give antibiotics every three hours for seventy-two hours (with the alarm clock set). I followed her directions, and he was soon better. He was also to avoid soy products. She told me to try a hot bath and give a baby aspirin for his wheezing attacks. It worked extremely well; we do it when any of the children has a bad cold. She suggested a dehumidifier in the basement, no carpet on his floor, no smoking in the house, using bleach on any mildew in the house (i.e. bathroom, garage door, etc.). We still do all of those things today.

I kept my last three babies on her mashed food diet, and they have had no problems with food allergies or asthma. We also drink water—no juice, milk, or soda pop between meals. It has kept them from having any burning with urination.

We truly love Dr. Denmark. My children say it's like going to see a wonderful grandma. An office visit is a great spiritual experience. She takes the time to go over life, childrearing, and the wisdom of her many years with us.

—Celeste Frey
Cumming, Georgia

My first time meeting Dr. Denmark occurred when my daughter was nine months old. I was searching for a miracle for Dixie, a way out of putting tubes in her ears. The idea scared me; it seemed unnatural to put foreign objects in the body and expect them to be accepted. At four weeks Dixie went on a bottle because I dried up trying to breast feed a ten-pound baby. That's when the infections started—every two weeks we were in the doctor's office changing medicines because the last one didn't work. She got yeast infections from them. According to the dentist, violent throwing up and horrible fevers later on caused the enamel on her molars to crack.

The child had been through enough. It was time to find a doctor who would determine the cause, not just keep precribing medicine after medicine. I learned of Dr. Denmark through my sister-in-law whose children had problems with rashes. On our very first visit she spent an hour with us and explained everything she was doing and why.

Gone were all dairy products, fruit juices, and sugar. If you had told me that just changing our way of eating would affect a child's ears, I would said you were crazy. But it works; it really does! In three days we had a brand new Dixie, and she has never been bothered with ear infections again.

I pray the good Lord will send someone to study with her and pick up where she leaves off. Thanks, Dr. Denmark, you saved another child!

—Jannette Williams
Canton, Georgia

When All Else Fails

D r. Denmark's a national treasure. Tom and I were blessed with twins on April 5, 1994. Our children were conceived by invitro fertilization after three years of fertility therapy. At the tender age of forty-two, I finally gave birth. Unfortunately the babies were eight weeks early. Thomas Justus weighed four and a half pounds, while our Alexandra Justine weighed only three and a half. Alex had no medical problems except for her weight and stayed in the preemie nursery for a month. Thomas, however, had trouble.

A tiny valve in his heart didn't close completely. The theory is that it caused him to be without enough oxygen. The magnificent human body manages such a situation by robbing secondary organs, so an inch of his small intestine went without adequate oxygen for a short time, causing his tummy to puff up. Thank God for our neonatologist who caught it early. Thomas required surgery at one week of age to remove the affected part of his small intestine. Only four days after his healthy sister, he came home with an ileostomy—the ends of the intestine are exposed, and the baby eliminates feces into a bag. After only six weeks, he had gained enough weight to merit further surgery to be "reconnected." All went well, or so we thought, until we were packed up to go home and discovered that Thomas had developed a fistula from a torn internal stitch. A third surgery was scheduled to fix it. He responded well, and we were finally able to take him home.

Our baby was now having a normal bowel movement but developed a bleeding diaper rash. The sweet child had already endured so much; it was just awful to see him in continuing pain. All the specialists felt it would just go away. They half-heartedly suggested a dozen different remedies from leaving his diaper off (can you imagine!) to various salves. Nothing helped. Thomas was in misery. One afternoon in Kroger's I ran into an ICU nurse from Northside Hospital who had taken care of our daughter. I begged her for advice.

"When all else fails, you go see Dr. Denmark," she said immediately. Being a hospital based speech therapist, I had heard of her. The next morning my mother and I took Thomas to see her. She told us right off that if he was eliminating feces after every feeding, he was allergic to his formula (a high-priced specialty one). She recommended soy formula and wrote me a prescription for sulfa cream. His little bottom was burned, but he should be well in four days. After three months of watching him suffer, it was just what we needed to hear and she was totally right. She also gave me a stern talking-to about structuring my routine—feeding, sleeping, bathing, and basically enjoying my life and babies. She stressed the need for a baby's stomach to empty before filling it again and how important it is not to be seduced into thinking they're are hungry just because they are crying. I should give them their last bottles at 10:00 p.m. and put them to bed for the night. At that point I was so exhausted I felt I was falling backwards when I wasn't. On the schedule she recommended, both babies were sleeping through the night, happy and calm during the day, and always healthy. Thus began my new life! What started off as tiny premies suddenly blossomed into big fat babies! At nine months Thomas weighs twenty-five pounds and is "off the chart." We laugh that he looks like a miniature linebacker! Alex weighs twenty pounds and is in the seventy-fifth percentile.

Dr. Denmark is the grandmother, doctor, and neighbor everyone deserves. We take the children back for checkups, and for ten dollars a visit we get counseling as well as sound medical advice! We leave feeling all is right with the world because of her positive attitude toward family, work, and love. She's hilarious. She told me a cow could raise her children better than I do because she doesn't have a brain to confuse her the way I allow mine to do. She told me to *think*. She stressed that I know what to do and should just go home and do it. That's what makes Dr. Denmark so special. She truly believes in the competence of parents—more so than we do. By empowering us, she knows we'll be better able to care for our children. As she so aptly put it, she can't afford to retire because she has too many parents to whip into shape. I'm grateful to be one of the many to say, "Thank you, Dr. Denmark."

—Justine Glover
Cumming, Georgia

Danielle had constant ear infections. By the time she was two, we joked with her doctor that she should get "frequent flyer" status for all the fifty-dollar visits we were making. She was also on the most expensive antibiotic, Ceclor (another fifty dollars a pop) which didn't always work. With one to two infections a month, it was terrible for all of us.

Six months later we moved to Cumming and heard about Dr. Denmark. She told us simply to get her off milk and the infections would stop. Sure enough, she's six now, and there hasn't been another. I ran into her old pediatrician and related this to him. His response was, "She was two years old and that's when kids tend to grow out of them anyway." What a closed mind to the value of proper eating!

—Eric and Tiffany Moen
Suwanee, Georgia

At 12:06 p.m. on April 17, 1993, my only son, Michael Taylor Cromer was born. He was a healthy eight pounds, thirteen ounces and twenty-two inches long. I was told by the hospital nurses always to lay him on his side or back. When we returned to the pediatrician for his two-month check up, he noticed a flat spot on the back of his head. The pediatrician told me to begin to rotate him from side to side and bring him back in a month. If the flat spot had not shaped up, he would send us to a surgeon who would reposition the bones in his head that had grown together. Needless to say, I stood there in total shock. I did not know what to do except pray and cry.

Two friends from church had been trying to get me to go to Dr. Denmark, but I was skeptical because of her age. Well, after I was told what I was told by that pediatrician, I was willing to try anything. So I called my friend at church and asked her to please take me there. Dr. Denmark checked my son out and said that he was perfectly healthy. Naturally, this relieved me of a major burden. She told me not to ever let anyone cut on my child's head. I was to begin placing him on his stomach and as he grew older his head would reshape itself naturally. Today my son is nineteen months old, and you cannot see any sign of the flat spot.

I thank God for Dr. Denmark. She has saved us lots of money and tears. She made me feel I could be a mother without the help of a doctor. I would recommend her to anybody!

—Jenny Cromer
Buford, Georgia

From Afar

Dr. Denmark is the wisest person I've ever known. Just being in the same room with her is like being with an angel.

She told us to change Nicholas' diaper with him lying on his tummy! It works!! It was easier to clean him and we didn't get sprayed. When he was born, the hospital told us to put him on his side to sleep. Other people told us to keep him on his back. Dr. Denmark's advice made the most sense to us. She said to place four bath towels under the crib sheet and keep him on his tummy. We followed Dr. Denmark's advice and our son had a beautifully shaped head. We never worried that he would suffocate because the towels gave him enough ventilation, should he sleep face down. He also had great control of his head at an early age because lying on his tummy gave him the ability to turn it from side to side.

We started out with a pediatrician close to home and would see Dr. Denmark (an hour away) from time to time. After just a few visits we realized that her words of wisdom, sixty-five years of experience, and godly attitude made the long drive worth it! Now when Nicholas is sick, we go straight to Dr. Denmark's! She truly loves children, and in my opinion, she is the best doctor in the world. I love her to death!

—Melanie Y. Doris
Fayetteville, Georgia

I grew up on Glenridge Drive near where Dr. Denmark had her office. I now have five children from one month to eight years old. Though we live in Dallas, I have never taken my children to a doctor here. I go back to Atlanta often, and we see Dr. Denmark. We were home this Christmas and took her our newest. After nursing my other four I thought, no big deal. He looks like all the others, so he'll be like they were. But at five weeks, he only weighed eight pounds, thirteen ounces less than at birth. Dr. Denmark said I was starving him and told me how to get him on a schedule, nursing first and then bottle feeding. I now have a baby who sleeps through the night and is perfectly healthy.

I home school my children and treasure the practical advice and love she gives. Because of Dr. Denmark, six-year-old Mary-Elsye wants to be a baby doctor with her office next to Dr. Denmark's. In case there's a question, she can run over and ask her!

We called her even on a ski trip to Colorado for my husband, who we thought was very ill. The Denmark Milk-of-Magnesia treatment worked wonders. He even shared it with the CEO of his company while they were in New York on business. The man thought he was crazy, but it was that or the emergency room. He chose the treatment and is now a believer. The lives she has touched are many. I thank God so much for her.

—Jan P. Winchester

Copell, Texas

As a missionary living in a foreign country, I have a very special place in my heart for Dr. Denmark and her advice for raising children. I first became acquainted with her after the birth of my first child. We were living in California at the time, but a friend of mine in the Atlanta area told me about the "revolutionary" ideas and concepts that Dr. Denmark had to offer in her book. In an age of "demand feeding and free living," her advice certainly seemed something new. We realized her "plan" was based on Biblical principals and good old-fashioned common sense. We chose to follow her advice, and her book became an invaluable source of information for us. We traveled the United States for a year and a half before coming to the mission field, and *Every Child Should Have a Chance* was a constant companion, helping us to give our daughter the greatest opportunity to learn and grow.

Our second child was born overseas, and we again sought encouragement and advice in the pages of Dr. Denmark's book. We owe her a great deal and praise God that He has allowed us the privilege of knowing such a dedicated and loving person. Thank you, Dr. Denmark, for your influence in our lives and the lives of our children.

—Pam Campbell
Argentina

Thank God!

Not once but twice has Dr. Denmark helped my daughter. The first time was in 1994, when five-year-old Danielle was on antibiotics and inhalers for croup. We spent hundreds of dollars, but after eleven days, she wasn't much better.

I heard Dr. Denmark was still in practice and immediately called her. To put it mildly, not only did she cure my daughter in three days, she told me what was wrong with me during my pregnancy after five obgyn's couldn't diagnose the problem. I had been bed-ridden with Danielle for six months, and told only various things that were incorrect. I told Dr. Denmark my symptoms, and she said right off, no question about it, I had had *placenta previa*. She charged me only eight dollars—after we had already spent so much. The second time she blessed us was this year when Danielle was rushed to Scottish Rite Emergency with fever, rash, croup,and vomiting. We spent six and a half hours in the waiting room, and they wouldn't allow her to eat or drink. At last the pediatrician came in for ten minutes max to tell us the strep test was negative but they would do another one. He gave her antibiotics for two days and said they'd get back to us. Well, Danielle kept getting worse and finally after eight calls, they told me the test was again negative. I went immediately to Dr. Denmark, and after only ten minutes found out Danielle had a severe case of scarlet fever! She could have died! I cried my eyes out all the way home, thanking God I'd gotten her to Dr. Denmark just in time.

Danielle was well in three days! Dr. Denmark is an angel. My daughter remains well and hopefully we will not have to take her tonsils out because of having such a severe case of scarlet fever. She had all the symptoms. If I just had gotten her to Dr. Denmark the first day, she would not have suffered so. My husband is still fighting the hospital bill over their misdiagnosis. We may still have to pay, even though they didn't treat her life-threatening disease properly. When we returned to Dr. Denmark for a follow up, she couldn't believe how quickly Danielle had recovered.

"This is a miracle," she said. "These glands aren't even swollen!!" I just cried with joy, hugged her, and thanked her up and down! God bless this lovely lady who really cares for our children.

—Diane Leonhardt
Marietta, Georgia

The first time I ever heard Dr. Denmark's name was in 1980 when I was expecting my first child. Friends who were also just starting their families mentioned her while discussing how to choose a pediatrician. I was amazed to hear of the incredible woman who, in her eighties at the time, was still practicing medicine and getting rave reviews from everyone who knew her. I came to find that you don't just "know" Leila Denmark, you "experience" her! I was encouraged on all sides to select this wise doctor. But thinking she certainly wouldn't be around much longer and wanting to be practical, I found a younger physician, . Fifteen years later, she's still going strong. By the way, my previous pediatrician quit his practice seven years ago to go into hospital administration! I probably would never have met Dr. Denmark had it not been for a crisis that struck our family in 1990.

It was mid-October when my husband developed a deep and troubling cough. It got progressively worse, but stoic that he is, Brent chose not to see a doctor and just ride it out. A couple of weeks later he and his brother left for a two-week trip to Germany, where the cough grew worse. That same night, almost-two-year-old Abigail began a dry, irritated cough that didn't alarm me at first. As the days went on it got worse. Soon she was waking up in the middle of the night with spasms that lasted for ten or fifteen minutes and ended with gagging and choking. One afternoon during her nap, my oldest son rushed downstairs to tell me that Abby was choking and turning blue in her crib. I found her as she was recovering from what I later discovered was a seizure. I immediately took her to our family physician, who diagnosed the problem as sinus drainage. Though she had no other indications, he prescribed Tylenol with codeine to help her sleep at night (no lie). Needless to say, I wasn't satisfied but didn't know what else to do. Deciding against the Tylenol "treatment," I chose to wait and see how the next few days went. She had no other symptoms and didn't seem to feel bad or be in any immediate danger. My husband was due home then and could help determine what to do. Her cough continued to worsen considerably, and after another middle-of-the-night spell, I checked our medical books to see what I could find out. I literally went cold at what I read. She probably had whooping cough, a childhood disease especially dangerous for those under two. We also had a newborn son who had started coughing.

Over the years I had heard about Dr. Denmark's work in developing the pertussis vaccine, research that undoubtedly has saved thousands of children from its ravages. If anyone could recognize the disease, it would be Dr. Denmark. I called her office, and much to my surprise she answered her own phone.

"Has she run a fever?" she asked. She hadn't. I was relieved, thinking maybe I was wrong after all.

"Well, she probably has whooping cough. Bring her in immediately," came the shocking reply.

We arrived at her quaint country office, where she ushered us in the back door so as not to infect those in the waiting room. Abby started coughing during the examination. She began to lose her breath, turned blue, and suddenly went limp. Her eyes rolled back in her head and her body began to convulse. I stood with our six other children looking on helplessly and begging Dr. Denmark to do something. It seemed hours before she began to come out of the seizure characteristic of whooping cough. All the while, Dr. Denmark was calm and controlled, talking to Abby and encouraging me at the same time. She quickly confirmed my fears, saying it was a classic case. She wished she could take her to the Medical College of Georgia in Augusta to teach the students what it looked like. Apparently, there was a tremendous amount of misdiagnosis going on. How well I knew!

After Abby had recovered from the seizure, Dr. Denmark explained why she had spent so long seeking a way to fight pertussis. In one week's time back in the 40s, she had helplessly watched three children in one family die of the disease that took thousands of lives before the days of vaccines and antibiotics. I was stunned by her story and feared deeply for my little girl. Then three-month-old Josiah started coughing. She asked how long he'd had it.

"Well, if he lives through the week, he'll probably make it," she replied casually, as if predicting a thunderstorm. I was paralyzed with terror at her words, but she gave me a prescription for an antibiotic and detailed instructions on administering it. The drive home is a blank. I do remember imagining preparations to bury my two youngest children.

I called my husband, who had just arrived home the day before. Word traveled fast through our church and circles of friends. They began prayers and started organizing. For the next three weeks we would spend night after night medicating the children every three hours and sitting with them while they coughed out all their air, turned blue, and vomited. As they gasped for breath, we heard the characteristic "whoop" for which the disease is named. I phoned Dr. Denmark every day with my questions and fears.

"I'm so glad you called. How's the baby?" she'd ask. What a blessing to hear her reassuring voice telling me I was doing fine treating them and that it simply took time to get them out of the woods. A lot of naysayers insisted our children should go into the hospital, have respiratory therapy, be on all sorts of medicine, even that I take them to a "real" doctor. Each time a suggestion came, I called Dr. Denmark and in a roundabout way asked what she thought.

"Honey, you're listening to your friends again," was her answer. "Just follow my instructions, and don't worry about what others say." She always ended our conversations with, "And have a good time." I've yet to figure out what she could possibly have meant by that!

During this time Dr. Denmark's husband was suffering from congestive heart failure, and she was caring for him at home . They had been married for over sixty years, I think, and it must have been agonizing for her to watch him deteriorate before her eyes. Yet she never once made me feel as if my frantic calls were any sort of nuisance. Just the opposite was true. Her compassion poured out upon our family in the midst of what must have been the heaviest trial of her life. He died just as our little ones were beginning to recover. I believe God used her to save the lives of our precious children. We'll be forever grateful for the unselfish and sacrificial way in which she gave herself to our household. There will never be another like her.

—Laura L. George
Woodstock, Georgia

Coming Home

There are many wonderful things I could say about Dr. Denmark, but I'd like to tell you about one incident still very clear in my heart and mind. My two-year-old son was very ill with a fever of 104 degrees one cold, windy night. When I called Dr. Denmark around ten o'clock, she told me to come to her office and she would meet us there. You can't imagine the feeling I had when we came up the hill to her precious little farmhouse-turned-office and saw the waiting light burning brightly for us. All the world seemed dark except that welcoming window. I couldn't help crying with relief at how comforting it felt to be heading to our caring Dr. Denmark. She greeted us in her little robe and slippers, and we gratefully placed our son in her loving arms. In a time when it's sometimes difficult to feel welcome in this world, being at Dr. Denmark's is just about as close to "coming home" as you can get! We love her so!

—Jodi Zorzi
Woodstock, Georgia

Biographical Sketch:

Leila Daughtry-Denmark, M.D.

By Steve Bowman

Born in Bulloch County, Georgia, on February 1, 1898, Leila Daughtry grew up on farmland granted to her family by the king of England several generations before her birth. Her grandmother had two daughters, one being Alice Cornelia Hendricks, Leila's mother. At the age of eighteen she married Mr. Elerbee Daughtry.

When Leila was born, the third oldest of twelve children, her family lived on a four-hundred-acre farm with an assortment of animals and crops. Their cash crop was cotton. She was six when their home burned. They had to live in a hastily constructed shanty until another, larger house was completed.

Both farm and home were run in a scheduled, orderly manner without fussing, fighting, or parental bickering. Leila's memories are of harmony, mutual help, and agreeable family relationships. Household workers assisted in child care and other duties. She recalls that the children of the black and white families who worked together on the farm were equally well-behaved.

Her parents taught their children primarily by example. There were no discussions of sex and alcohol or stern warnings when she went on dates. Her parents set standards that she sought to emulate. "You get apples off apple trees," she is fond of saying. "If my mother had raised her voice, I'd have raised mine. If I'd seen my mother smoking, I probably would have, too. But I never saw any of that." The even-tempered Daughtrys practiced genteel manners.

Leila's father was a self-educated, well-read Southern gentleman who was always dressed meticulously. He managed the farm operations without doing any of the manual labor. Elected mayor of Portal, he served in that capacity for thirty-five years. Alice Daughtry died of cancer at the age of forty-five when their youngest son was only two and a half years old. Elerbee later remarried.

Leila attended the two-room schoolhouse a couple of miles from home, but she didn't begin until she was eight. Before then she couldn't walk fast enough to keep up with her older sisters.

The young Leila often pondered what life work she might pursue. Greatly admiring hat makers, who were viewed as artists, she taught herself the craft. Next came sewing lessons and the desire to be a clothing designer. After that she learned to cook and was certain she would be a dietitian.

Leila went to high school in Statesboro at the First District Agricultural and Mechanical School on the campus of what later became Georgia Southern University, not far from her home in Portal. At Tift College in Forsyth, her classmates called her "Doc," probably because of her interest in anatomy and dissection. (Tift was located in the city of Forsyth, not Forsyth County.)

During her college years Leila read a book on India that detailed the need for medical personnel in that country. She decided to become a missionary doctor to the women of India, where taboos prohibited their being examined by male doctors. A life of medical service out there would suit her just fine. However, a growing interest in a certain young man by the name of John Eustace Denmark changed her plans! They had known each other from childhood but were never romantically linked. After four years at Tift she and Eustace were engaged. As she tells it: "No one would have me, and no one would have him, so we teamed up!" Deciding to teach school in order to pay her debts before marrying, she gave up the idea of becoming a doctor.

Her first job was in Acworth, northwest of Atlanta. She was to teach science in the local high school. Having grown up in a peaceful, orderly home environment, Leila Daughtry was in no way prepared for the challenges of a public school system.

"Miss Daughtry, you're going to teach the meanest kids on earth," warned the professor who met her at the station. She had no idea what he meant but soon found out. Some of the boys in her class were better than six feet tall, strong and unruly. At one hundred pounds, she was no match for them: On the first day she defused a tense situation by requesting the boys' help in setting up and breaking down the classroom. During her nine-month stay she never had any trouble with them; they became her friends.

Realizing she didn't want teaching to be her lifetime occupation, she gave it up after another year in Claxton. At this time Eustace received an appointment to Java, Indonesia, as vice-consul in the city of Soerabaya. He secured her promise to wait for him. The two year assignment put their marriage plans on hold and allowed the eager Miss Daughtry to set her sights on entering medical school in August. But first she decided to attend Mercer University in Macon to take the prerequisite physics and chemistry. They told her the courses were so difficult that she might as well not attempt them. She wasn't to be deterred.

When she later applied at the Medical College of Georgia in Augusta, she found all the places were filled; she would have to reapply the following year. She asked them to reconsider their decision. They did so, allowing her to enter the program. Eustace returned from Java in 1926, and Leila completed her degree two years later.

The year 1928 was a busy one for the young couple. They married in the Baptist Church in Portal, on June 11 at high noon so all the farmers could attend and then return to the fields. "We married on Monday. I cooked breakfast on Tuesday and started work at Grady Hospital in Atlanta," Dr. Denmark reminisces. She began her internship in the segregated black wards under Dr. Hines Roberts. In August of that year he asked her to join the staff of Henrietta Egleston Hospital for Children. She became the institution's first intern, admitting its first patient.

During that time Central Presbyterian Church opened a charity baby clinic. She was one of many physicians who donated time to it every week. Two years later, Leila followed Dr. Roberts to Philadelphia Children's Hospital for six months before returning to Egleston and Central Presbyterian. She would continue her work there for the next fifty-six years.

When Mary, their only child, was born in 1931, they set up a clinic in their home on Highland Avenue so she could both care for the baby and see patients. It was during this time that they joined the Druid Hills Baptist Chruch, where Dr. Denmark still keeps her membership. Next they moved to Hudson Drive in the Highland-Virginia neighborhood and lived there until 1949 when they moved again to Glenridge Drive in Sandy Springs. At the time this was very much in the country. Their fifty-two acres afforded privacy and solace from the crowded city. In 1985 the couple made their final move to Alpharetta.

Her beloved Eustace passed away in 1990 with congenital heart failure. His death was a heavy blow, but she continued on with her practice. At the age of 103 she still maintains a full work load, seeing patients in a 150-year-old farmhouse next door to her home.

Published in 1971, *Every Child Should Have a Chance* puts forth her basic philosophy of childrearing and has sold thousands of copies around the world. Numerous articles and documentaries by local and national TV have highlighted her work. More than anything, the multitude of children she has successfully treated give testimony to the usefulness of her life.

History records that Leila Daughtry Denmark's greatest accomplishment was her contribution to the development of the pertussis vaccine, to which she devoted eleven years of research. It reveals much about this remarkable woman that she says, "My greatest accomplishment was getting Eustace as a husband. He's the one who enabled me to practice medicine without thinking of money. He helped get me through medical school and allowed me to continue my work at home while rearing Mary. Without him I could never have done what I have, helping rich or poor who couldn't otherwise get help. There are none too poor or too rich to take care of their children. They just needed to be shown how," she concludes. Few people have ever come close to Leila Daughtry Denmark in providing a loving, helping hand to so many parents.

Special Services and Studies

- Member of pediatrics staff of Grady Hospital, Atlanta
- Member of staff of Central Presbyterian Church Baby Clinic, Atlanta, 1928 to 1983, devoting one day each week to this charity
- Member of staff, Henrietta Egleston Hospital for Children, Atlanta
- Extensive research in diagnosis, treatment and immunization of whooping cough over a period of eleven years, beginning in 1933. Papers covering these studies were published in *American Journal of Diseases of Children* (a publication of the American Medical Association) in September 1936 and March 1942
- Author of a book on child care, *Every Child Should Have a Chance*, 1971. Second edition, 1977; third edition, 1982. Now in its sixth printing

Memberships and Honors:

- American Medical Association
- Medical Association of Georgia
- Georgia Chapter, American Academy of Pediatrics (honorary president)
- Medical Association of Atlanta
- Druid Hills Baptist Church, Atlanta
- Selected as Atlanta's Woman of the Year, 1953
- Received distinguished service citation from Tift College, April 14, 1970, as "a devout humanitarian who has invested her life in pediatric services to all families without respect to economic status, race, or national origin.... Devoted humanitarian, doctor *par excellence*, generous benefactor."
- Honorary degree, doctor of humanities, Tift College, June 4, 1972
- Fisher Award in 1935 for outstanding research in diagnosis, treatment, and immunization of whooping cough
- Distinguished Alumni Award from Georgia Southern College, Statesboro, January 28, 1978
- Honorary president, Georgia Chapter, American Academy of Pediatrics
- Community Service Award for 1980, sponsored by television station WXIA, Atlanta
- Distinguished Alumni Award from Mercer University, Macon, 1980
- Distinguished Alumni Award from Tift College, Forsyth, 1980
- Book of Golden Deeds Award, Buckhead Exchange Club, Atlanta, April 17, 1981
- Citation from Citizens of Portal at Turpentine Festival, October 16, 1982, jointly with husband, John Eustace Denmark, for outstanding achievement and service
- Medal of Honor from Daughters of the American

Revolution, Joseph Habersham chapter, Atlanta,
October 20, 1983
- Selected as member of Gracious Ladies of Georgia,
  Columbus, 1987
- Distinguished Alumni Award from Medical College of
  Georgia, May 2, 1987
- Honored with husband by Mercer University as life member
  of President's Club, December 4, 1987
- Shining Light Award, Atlanta Gas Light Company, 1989
- Honorary degree, Doctor of Science, Mercer University,
  June 2, 1991
- Honorary degree, Doctor of Science, Emory University,
  May, 2000
- Heroes, Saints and Legends Award, Wesley Woods, 2000

Index